SRA
Reading Mastery®
Transformations

Reading
Textbook A

Siegfried Engelmann

Susie Andrist

Tina Wells

Acknowledgments

The authors are extremely grateful to Tina Wells for keeping the ship afloat on this project, and to Patricia McFadden, Margie Mayo, and Chris Gladfelter for their great attention to detail.

CREDITS

Stephanie's Ponytail
"Stephanie's Ponytail" copyright © 1996 Bob Munsch Enterprises Ltd. (text)/Michael Martchenko (art). First published by Annick Press, Ltd. All rights reserved. Reproduced by permission.

George at the Zoo
George at the Zoo by Sally George, illustration by Rob Mancini. Text copyright 1994 by Sally George, illustration copyright 1994 by Rob Mancini. Reproduced with the permission of Cengage Learning Australia Pty. Ltd.

Remember
"Remember" is used by permission of the poet, Pamela Mordecai.

PHOTO CREDITS

2 Brand X/SuperStock; **18** (tl)Scott Bauer, USDA Natural Resources Conservation Service, (tr)©Corbis/Glow Images, (bl)©Pixtal/age fotostock, (br)Chris Willig; **32** (tl)Life On White/Getty Images, (tr)©Ingram Publishing/Alamy, (bc)Javier Larrea/Pixtal/age fotostock, (bl)David Broberg/iStock/Getty Images, (br)Hashim Pudiyapura/Getty Images, (tc)Rodrigo A. Torres/Glow Images; **36** (tr)Arthur Baensch/Corbis/Getty Images, (tc)©Ingram Publishing/Alamy, (tl)Javier Larrea/Pixtal/age fotostock, (bl)Rodrigo A. Torres/Glow Images, (br)Hashim Pudiyapura/Getty Images, (bc)Javier Larrea/Pixtal/age fotostock; **39** Frizi/iStock/Getty Images; **40** Max Dereta/Photodisc/Getty Images; **45** Amos Morgan/Getty Images; **55** (l)©Mjdphoto/Alamy, (cl)©Ingram Publishing/Alamy, (c,r)Ken Cavanagh/McGraw-Hill Education, (cr)Richard Hutchings/McGraw-Hill Education; **83** (l)©Mjdphoto/Alamy, (r)©Ingram Publishing/Alamy, (cl)Richard Hutchings/McGraw-Hill Education, (c)Ken Cavanagh/McGraw-Hill Education, (cr)McGraw-Hill Education; **104** (t)Jason Edwards/Media Bakery, (c)T. Kitchin & V. Hurst/NHPA, (b)George Bernard/NHPA; **105** T. Kitchin & V. Hurst/NHPA; **107** (cr)Pixtal/age fotostock, (l,cl,r)Rick Hoblitt/USGS; **118** (tl)Akimasa Harada/Getty Images, (tc)©Ingram Publishing/Alamy, (tr)G.K. & Vikki Hart/Getty Images, (bl)McGraw-Hill Education, (bc)Tetra Images/Alamy, (br)Vladan Milisavljevic/E+/Getty Images; **120** (tl)D. Hurst/Alamy, (tc)Laura Perlick/U.S. Fish & Wildlife Service, (tr)Morley Read/iStock/Getty Images, (bl)Watcha/iStock/Getty Images, (bc)Herman Bresser/Moment/Getty Images, (br)TheLionRoar/iStock/Getty Images; **122** Marcin Pawinski/iStock/Getty Images; **128** (t)Comstock Images/Alamy, (c,b)McGraw-Hill Education; **129** (t,b)Photo 24/age fotostock; **134** (l)Dot Box Inc./McGraw-Hill Education, (r)Mark Steinmetz/McGraw-Hill Education; **135** (tl)Vasiliy Vishnevskiy/Hemera/Getty Images, (tcl)Juniors/SuperStock, (tcr)Techin24/iStock/Getty Images, (tr)Comstock Images/Alamy, (bl)eve_eve01genesis/iStock/Getty Images, (bcl)GlobalP/iStock/Getty Images, (bcr)HueyJ/iStock/Getty Images, (br)Jurij Zherebtsov/Hemera/Getty Images; **165** Ingram Publishing/SuperStock; **168** (l)Margo Harrison/Hemera/Getty Images, (r)Anna Yakimova/123RF; **176** (l)©Vasiliy Vishnevskiy/Alamy, (c)Vasiliy Vishnevskiy/Hemera/Getty Images, (r)Jurij Zherebtsov/Hemera/Getty Images; **183** H. Peter/Alamy; **184** (tr)Vasiliy Vishnevskiy/Hemera/Getty Images, (tcr)Juniors/SuperStock, (tcl)Techin24/iStock/Getty Images, (bcl)Comstock Images/Alamy, (tl)eve_eve01genesis/iStock/Getty Images, (bl)GlobalP/iStock/Getty Images, (br)Hugh Jelen/iStock/Getty Images, (bcr)Jurij Zherebtsov/Hemera/Getty Images; **201** H. Peter/Alamy; **203** jhofoto/iStock/Getty Images; **209** (l,r)McGraw-Hill Education; **226** (tl)©Foodcollection, (tc)©Goodshoot/Alamy, (tr)©D. Hurst/Alamy, (bl)©Mark Dierker/McGraw-Hill Education; **233** (l)magone/123RF, (r)pandemin/iStock/Getty Images; **241** David Planchet; **246** (tl)Fotosonline/Alamy, (tc)©Richard Carey/Alamy, (tr,bcl)G.K. & Vikki Hart/Getty Images, (bl)John Montenieri/CDC, (bcr)leoba/123RF, (br)Hashim Pudiyapura/Getty Images; **251** (c)John Montenieri/CDC, (cl)G.K. & Vikki Hart/Getty Images, (l)Hashim Pudiyapura/Getty Images, (cr)Purestock/SuperStock, (r)Jim Peaco/NPS; **258** H. Peter/Alamy; **259** (tc,c)McGraw-Hill Education, (tl)Michael H/Getty Images, (b)Ken Karp/McGraw-Hill Education, (tr)blackwaterimages/Getty Images; **260** (tr,bl)G.K. & Vikki Hart/Getty Images, (bc)Purestock/SuperStock, (tl)Ingram Publishing/Alamy, (bcl)Eric Isselee/123RF, (bcr)Carson Ganci/age fotostock, (br)Matti Suopajarvi/mattisj/Getty Images.

mheducation.com/prek-12

Send all inquiries to:
McGraw-Hill Education
8787 Orion Place
Columbus, OH 43240

ISBN: 978-0-07-905409-8
MHID: 0-07-905409-9

Printed in the United States of America.

2 3 4 5 6 7 8 9 10 LWI 26 25 24 23 22 21

Table of Contents

Table of Contents

A

1

1. rule
2. page
3. people
4. tiger
5. striped
6. straight
7. title

2

1. water
2. living
3. through
4. sugar
5. item
6. skill

3

1. babies
2. flies
3. kittens
4. spiders
5. boxes
6. items

Living Things

Here is a rule about all living things: **All living things grow, and all living things need water.**

Are trees living things? Yes. So you know that trees grow and trees need water.

Dogs are living things. So do dogs grow? Do dogs need water?

People are living things. Do people grow? Do people need water?

Here is another rule about all living things: **All living things make babies.**

Trees are living things. So trees make baby trees.
Are fish living things? So what do fish make?
Are spiders living things? So what do spiders make?
Remember the rule: **All living things make babies.**

Number your paper from 1 through 13.

C INFORMATION ITEMS

1. What do all living things need?

2. What do all living things make?

3. Do all living things grow?

4. Are flies living things?

5. Write the letters of **3** things you know about flies.

   a. Flies need water.   d. Flies need ants.

   b. Flies need sugar.   e. Flies make babies.

   c. Flies grow.

6. Are dogs living things?

7. So you know that dogs need ▮▮▮▮ .

8. And you know that dogs make ▮▮▮▮ .

9. Are chairs living things?

10. Do chairs need water?

The Tiger and the Frog

Tom's brother had two pets. One pet was a frog. The other pet was a big mean tiger. Tom's brother kept his pets in boxes. One day Tom said, "I want to play with your pet frog."

Tom's brother said, "Here is the rule about where I keep that frog. **I keep the frog in the box that is striped.**" Then Tom's brother said, "Don't get mixed up, because I keep my pet tiger in one of the other boxes."

Tom said the rule to himself. Then he went into the room with the boxes.

Here is what Tom saw.

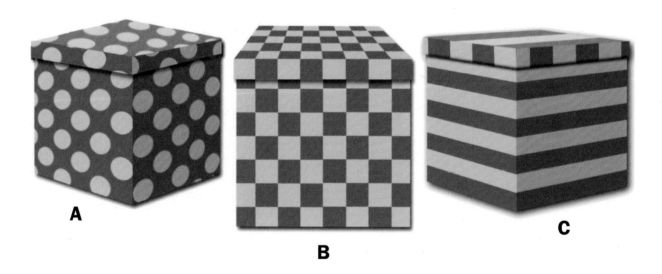

A

B

C

Tom looked at box A. He tried to think of the rule his brother had told him.

Is box A striped?

So is the frog inside box A?

Tom looked at box B.

Is box B striped?

So is the frog inside box B?

Tom looked at box C. After looking at all the boxes, Tom opened box B.

Did a frog hop out of box B?

Turn to the next page and you will see what happened.

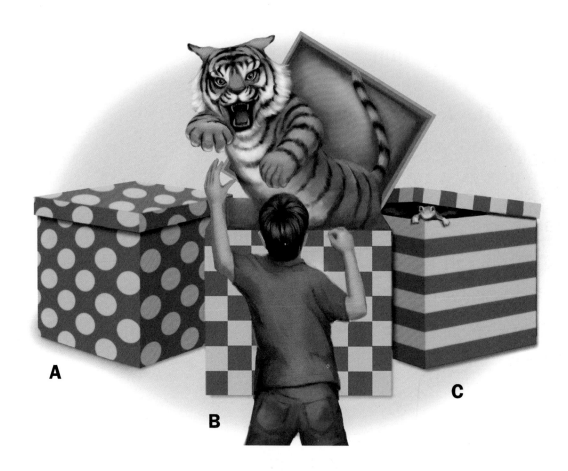

E STORY ITEMS

11. What's the title of today's story?
    - The Tiger and the Dog
    - The Tiger and the Frog
    - The Dog and the Frog

12. Name **2** pets that Tom's brother had.

13. Did Tom open the right box?

END OF LESSON 1

A

1

1. whole
2. moop
3. carry
4. covered
5. make-believe
6. facts
7. review

2

1. field
2. through
3. straight
4. straighter
5. forest
6. page

3

1. striped
2. pointed
3. wise
4. strange
5. color

Make-Believe Animals

Here's a real animal.

Here's a make-believe animal.

What part of the animal is make-believe?

The story you'll read today tells about animals called moops. Moops are make-believe animals. That means there are not really any moops.

Number your paper from 1 through 9.

C INFORMATION ITEMS

1. Write the letter of each make-belicve animal.

A

B

C

D

E

F

Bob and Don Find Moops

Don and Bob lived near a strange forest. There were many strange animals in the forest. One strange animal was a moop. Moops were little animals with long hair. They made very good pets.

One day Don and Bob went out to get pet moops. On the path through the forest they met a wise old man. The wise old man said, "A moop makes a good pet. But do not cut a moop's hair. Here's the rule about a moop: **The more you cut its hair, the faster its hair grows.**"

Don listened to the old man. But Bob did not listen.

Don found a pet moop, and Bob found a pet moop. Don took his pet moop home and put it in a box. Bob took his pet moop home and looked at it. Bob said, "The hair on this moop is too long. So I will cut it." Bob started to cut the moop's hair, but the hair started to grow back. So Bob cut more hair. But the more he cut the hair, the faster the hair grew.

Soon the moop's hair was so long that it filled the room. Soon the hair was so long that Bob could not find his moop.

Don kept his moop for years. Don had a lot of fun with his moop. But Bob did not have fun with his moop. He never found his moop. All he could see was a room full of hair.

THE END

2. What is the title of today's story?

    • Moops Find Bob and Don

    • Bob and Don Find Moops

    • Bob and Don Find Mops

3. Write the 2 missing words.

    The wise old man said, "The more you cut its ▬▬▬ , the ▬▬▬ its hair grows."

4. Who did not listen to the wise old man?

5. What happened to the moop's hair when Bob cut it?

6. Did Bob have fun with his moop?

7. Are moops **real** or **make-believe?**

8. One of the pictures shows Don's moop in a room. Write the letter of that picture.

9. One of the pictures shows Bob's moop in a room. Write the letter of that picture.

A   B   C   D

END OF LESSON 2

1

1. great
2. danger
3. destroy
4. grove
5. measure
6. weight

2

1. <u>bluer</u>
2. <u>together</u>
3. <u>facts</u>
4. <u>howled</u>
5. <u>branches</u>
6. <u>make</u>-believe

3

1. covered
2. washed
3. pointed
4. crashed
5. cracked

4

1. twig
2. during
3. carry
4. ground
5. bark

5

1. roots
2. trunk
3. whole
4. ripe
5. flowers
6. whiter

Trees

Trees have roots. The roots are under the ground. The roots do two things. The roots hold the tree up to keep it from falling over. The roots also carry water from the ground to all parts of the tree. Trees could not live if they did not have roots.

roots

PICTURE 1

Here's another fact about trees. Trees do not grow in the winter because the ground is cold. In the spring, trees start to grow. The sun makes the ground warmer in the spring. First the top of the ground gets warm. Then the deeper parts of the ground get warm.

PICTURE 2

Small trees begin to grow before big trees grow. Small trees grow first because their roots are not very deep in the ground. Their roots are in warmer ground. So their roots warm up before the roots of big trees warm up.

Number your paper from 1 through 17.

C INFORMATION ITEMS

1. What part of a tree is under the ground?

2. Roots keep the tree from ▨ .

3. Roots carry ▨ to all parts of the tree.

4. Could trees live if they didn't have roots?

5. When do trees begin to grow?
   - in the winter   • in the spring

6. Trees begin to grow when their roots get ▨ .

Look at these trees.

7. Write the letter of the tree that has deeper roots.

8. Write the letter of the tree that begins to grow first every year.

9. Which letter in the picture below shows where the ground gets warm first?

10. Which letter shows where the ground gets warm last?

Don Washes the White Spot

Don had a pretty white coat. But he didn't like white coats. He wanted a blue coat. Don said, "I'll buy a blue coat." So he started to walk to town. He had to walk through the strange forest to get to town. Don met the wise old man on the path through the forest. Don told the wise old man, "I'm on my way to get a blue coat."

The wise old man said, "I will give you a blue coat." The wise old man held up a pretty blue coat.

The coat had one little white spot on it. The old man pointed to the spot and said, "Do not try to wash this spot away. Here's the rule: **The more you wash this spot, the bigger it will get.**"

Don did not listen to the old man. Don took the pretty blue coat home. Then he said to himself, "I don't like that little spot on the coat. I will wash it away."

So Don got some soap and water. Then he started to wash the spot. He washed a little bit and the spot got a little bigger. Don washed some more. And the white spot got bigger. Don washed and washed and washed. And the spot got bigger and bigger and bigger. The more Don washed, the bigger the spot got.

Soon the white spot was so big that it covered the whole coat. The whole coat was white. Now Don did not have a white coat and a blue coat. He had two white coats. Don said, "I hate white coats."

THE END

11. What's the title of today's story?

    - Don Washes the Moop

    - Don Washes the White Spot

    - Don Spots the White Moop

12. Did Don like white coats?

13. The old man said, "The more you wash this spot, the ▮▮▮▮ it will get."

14. What color was the coat that the old man gave Don?

15. What happened to the spot when Don washed it?

16. What color was the coat after Don washed it?

17. Write the letter of the picture that shows a forest.

A

B

C

D

END OF LESSON 3

A

1
1. alive
2. seasons
3. terrible
4. millions
5. measure
6. weight
7. money

2
1. during
2. blowing
3. cheering
4. glowing
5. growing
6. lying

3
1. apple
2. loved
3. greatest
4. meaner
5. cracked
6. crashed

4
1. grove
2. bark
3. trunk
4. howled
5. branches
6. care

5
1. pretty
2. twig
3. ripe
4. flowers
5. Tina
6. destroy

Apple Trees

Apple trees are different from forest trees. Forest trees are tall and straight. Apple trees are short and not so straight. Forest trees have very small branches. Apple trees have large branches.

Here is a forest tree.

Here is an apple tree.

Apple trees have white flowers in the spring. Later, in the summer, a little apple starts growing from each place where there was a flower.

By the fall, the apples are big and ripe. They will fall off if they are not picked. The leaves also fall off in the fall. During the winter, the apple tree does not grow. It is in a kind of sleep. It will start growing again in the spring.

The pictures below show a twig of an apple tree in the spring, the summer, the fall, and the winter.

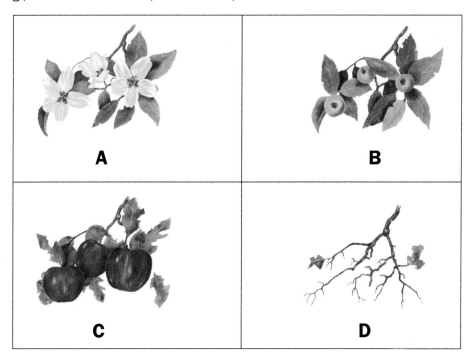

Number your paper from 1 through 17.

C INFORMATION ITEMS

1. What color are the flowers that apple trees make?
   - red
   - white
   - blue

2. When do those flowers come out?
   - fall
   - summer
   - spring

3. What grows in each place where there was a flower?

4. Which has a tall straight trunk, a forest tree or an apple tree?
   - forest tree
   - apple tree

5. Which has larger branches, a forest tree or an apple tree?
   - forest tree
   - apple tree

The Little Apple Tree

Tina was an apple tree. She loved to hold her leaves out to the sun. She loved to make green leaves and pretty white flowers in the spring. She loved to make big red apples in the fall. And she loved to have a great big sleep every winter.

But Tina didn't get to do all the things she loved to do. She didn't live in a nice grove of apple trees. She lived in a forest with big mean trees that didn't care about her. Those big trees took all of the sunshine they could reach. And they didn't leave much for Tina. They dropped leaves and bark and seeds and branches all over little Tina.

When the wind started blowing, the big trees would swing and howl and have lots of fun. They didn't let the wind reach Tina.

And those big trees didn't care what Tina said.

One spring day, she said, "Please stop dropping things on me. I am trying to make white flowers."

One of the big trees said, "She doesn't want us to do **this.**" That tree dropped a small branch right on Tina.

Another big tree said, "Ho, ho. She doesn't want us to do **this.**" That tree dropped a bigger branch on Tina.

The biggest tree said, "Ho, ho. She really doesn't want us to do **this.**" That tree dropped the biggest branch it had. That branch crashed down on top of Tina. It cracked two of Tina's branches.

The big trees howled and said, "That was good. We really dropped some big ones on that apple tree. Ho, ho."

MORE NEXT TIME

E STORY ITEMS

6. What's the title of today's story?
   - The Mean Trees
   - The Little Apple Tree
   - How Apples Grow

7. How many apple trees were near Tina?
   - 26   • none   • one

8. Who kept the wind and the sunshine away from Tina?
   - the wind   • the rain   • the tall trees

For items 9 through 12, read each thing that Tina did. Then write the season that tells when she did it.

- winter
- spring
- summer
- fall

9. Made big red apples

10. Made leaves and white flowers

11. Made little apples where each flower was

12. Went to sleep

13. Write 3 things the big trees dropped on Tina.

- bark
- apples
- flowers
- boxes
- branches
- leaves
- cans

The pictures show the same twig in 4 seasons. **Write the name of the season for each twig.**

14.   15.   16.   17.

END OF LESSON 4

A

1

1. true
2. sure
3. character
4. arrow
5. dead

2

1. <u>sea</u>sons
2. <u>cam</u>per
3. <u>mat</u>ter
4. <u>glow</u>ing
5. <u>grow</u>ing
6. <u>cur</u>ly

3

1. millions
2. greatest
3. blowing
4. knocked
5. meaner
6. arrows

4

1. orange
2. fence
3. agree
4. money
5. campfire
6. alive

5

1. animals
2. destroy
3. another
4. danger
5. terrible
6. cheering

Forest Fires

A forest is a place with lots of tall trees that are close together. The inside of a forest is very dark.

Sometimes, a forest burns. That's called a forest fire.

Here are facts about forest fires.

The danger of a forest fire is greatest when the trees and other plants are very dry.

The danger of a forest fire is not very great in the winter or spring. In these seasons things are wet and trees do not have dry leaves.

In the late summer and fall, the leaves die and become dry. Many dry leaves are on the ground in the fall. So if a small fire starts, it may grow larger as it moves through the dry leaves on the ground. Soon, that fire may leap up into the trees and become a terrible forest fire.

Forest fires kill animals and trees. Large forest fires may burn for weeks. They may destroy millions of trees. And it may take more than 200 years for the forest to grow back.

Number your paper from 1 through 15.

C INFORMATION ITEMS

1. In which seasons is the danger of forest fires greatest?
   - winter and spring
   - spring and summer
   - summer and fall
   - fall and winter
2. In the fall are the leaves on trees dead or alive?
   - dead
   - alive
3. Are dead leaves wet or dry?
   - wet
   - dry
4. In spring, are the leaves on trees dead or alive?
   - dead
   - alive
5. Are those leaves wet or dry?
   - wet
   - dry
6. A forest fire may burn for ___.
   - seasons
   - weeks
   - years
7. A forest fire kills ___ and ___.
   - plants
   - animals
   - fish
   - whales
8. About how many years could it take for the forest to grow back?
   - 100 years
   - 20 years
   - 200 years

Campers Come into the Forest

Tina was very sad all summer and all fall. The only thing the big trees let Tina do was sleep when winter came. They went to sleep too. But in the spring when Tina woke up and tried to make little green leaves, the big trees started dropping things and making jokes.

"That apple tree doesn't like it when we do **this**," they would say and then drop something on her.

Things were bad all spring and all summer.

On one fall day, the trees were meaner than ever. Tina had made lots of big red apples. The big trees were trying to drop branches on her and knock off her apples.

They would say, "She doesn't like it when we do **this**," and they would drop a branch. If the branch knocked off an apple, the big trees would cheer. This game went on until the big trees had no more branches they could let go of. Poor Tina had only three apples left.

Just then three campers came into the forest. They made a fire. The big trees got scared.

One big tree said, "What is the matter with those campers? Don't they know they should not make fires in the fall?"

Another big tree said, "Yes, things are dry. And we hate forest fires."

After a while, the campers put dirt on the fire and started to leave. They didn't see that part of the fire was still glowing.

"Oh, no," one of the trees said, as the campers were leaving. "That fire will start up as soon as the wind blows."

Another tree said, "And it will make a forest fire. And we will burn up."

MORE NEXT TIME

E STORY ITEMS

9. Did Tina feel happy or sad?
   - happy
   - sad

10. What did the big trees do to knock off her apples?
    - dropped boxes on her
    - yelled at her
    - dropped branches

11. How many apples did she have left at the end of the game?
    - 26
    - 3
    - 1

12. The big trees didn't knock off the rest of her apples because they didn't have any more ___ .
    - time
    - money
    - things to drop

13. Who came to the forest at the end of the game?
    - an apple tree
    - a goat
    - campers

14. What did the campers make?
    - a fire
    - a house
    - a hut

15. The big trees saw something the campers did not see. What was that?
    - Tina
    - a glowing fire
    - a hot rock

END OF LESSON 5

A

1

1. thousand
2. connect
3. touch
4. half
5. centimeter
6. unit
7. element

2

1. campfire
2. something
3. anything
4. sunshine
5. without

3

1. garden
2. age
3. show
4. shown
5. flames

4

1. remove
2. setting
3. camel
4. bonk

5

1. objects
2. agree
3. hump
4. feet
5. curly

6

1. waded
2. character
3. stream
4. plot
5. tadpole

Camels and Pigs

In the next lesson, you'll read about a camel and a pig. Camels and pigs are the same in some ways and different in some ways. Both camels and pigs have four feet.

Here's a pig's foot.   Here's a camel's foot.

The pig's nose and the camel's nose are different.

Which animal has this nose?

Which animal has this nose?

The back of each animal is different. One of the animals has a large hump on its back.

A camel's tail and a pig's tail are different. One animal has a long tail. The other animal has a short curly tail.

One of the animals is very big and the other animal is much, much smaller. Here they are, side by side.

Tina Is Happy

The trees were afraid of a forest fire. A campfire was glowing, and it would make flames as soon as the wind started blowing. The campers who made the fire were leaving. As they walked away, the big trees shouted at each other, "Drop something on those campers. Make them stop and go back."

But the trees didn't have anything to drop. They had dropped all their old branches and leaves on Tina. The campers were now walking under Tina's branches.

The big trees called, "Tina, save us. Save us. Drop something on those campers." ★

"Yes," a big tree said, "if you save us we'll be good to you for 100 years."

Tina hated to drop her only three apples, but she did. They landed on the campers: bonk, bonk, bonk. The campers stopped and bent over to pick up the apples.

One of the campers looked back at the fire and said, "We didn't put out that fire. Shame on us."

They went back and made sure that the fire was out before they left.

So now, Tina is happy. The big trees don't drop things on her. ☾ In the spring those trees bend far to the side so the sun can reach Tina.

Tina can make green leaves and pretty white flowers. If one of the big trees holds a branch out and keeps the sun from reaching her, the other big trees say, "Hey, move your branch. You're taking Tina's sunshine."

And in the fall, those trees are very proud when Tina makes apples—lots and lots of big red apples. "Look at all those apples," they say. "And we helped her make them. Good for us."

Those big trees agree about how much Tina did for them. They say, "Tina gave up her only three apples to save us, so we love that little apple tree."

THE END

Setting, Characters, Plot

All stories have three main elements. They are **the setting, the characters,** and **the plot.**

- The **setting** is where and when the story takes place.
- The **characters** are the people, animals, or objects that do things in the story.
- The **plot** is what happens to the characters in the story.

E INFORMATION ITEMS

Some of these parts belong to a **cow.** Some of them belong to a **camel.** And some belong to a **pig. Write the name of the animal that has the part shown in each picture.**

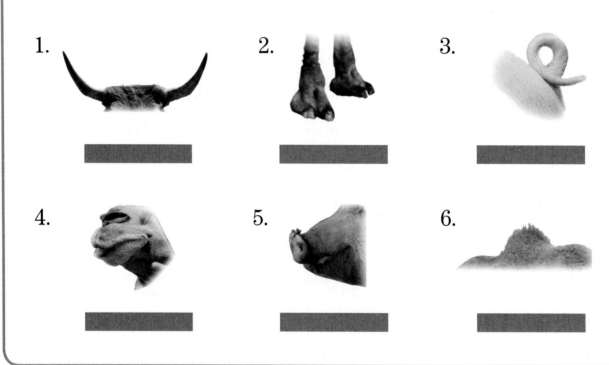

1.

2.

3.

4.

5.

6.

7. Which is bigger, a camel or a pig?

8. Which has a longer tail, a camel or a pig?

F STORY ITEMS

9. The big trees didn't drop something on the campers because they didn't have any more ▨ .

• time   • money   • things to drop

10. The big trees wanted someone to help them. Who was that?

    • a big tree   • a farmer   • Tina

11. The big trees told Tina that they would be good to her for ▮▮▮▮ years.

    • 30   • 100   • 500

12. How many apples did Tina have before she dropped some?

13. How many apples did she drop?

14. What did one camper see when he was picking up an apple?

    • the campfire   • Tina   • the tall trees

15. Did the campers put out the fire?

16. Do the big trees still do mean things to Tina?

17. Write the letters for the 2 things the big trees do to make sure that Tina gets lots of sun.

    a. move their branches so Tina gets sun

    b. make shadows

    c. drop bark and branches

    d. bend to the side

END OF LESSON 6

A

1
1. ce
2. ou
3. ir

2
1. ground
2. pound
3. around
4. race
5. place
6. fence

3
1. inside
2. without
3. flatter
4. ugliest
5. touching
6. wider

4
1. sure
2. easy
3. should
4. right
5. half
6. flat
7. gate

5
1. sharper
2. thousand
3. promise
4. centimeter
5. garden
6. people

More Facts About Camels

In today's lesson, you'll read about camels and pigs. Here are some facts about camels.

Most camels live in places that are very dry. Sometimes there is no rain for years in these places.

The camels work like trucks that carry things.

Camels do a good job because they can go for ten days without drinking water. That's because they can drink a lot of water at one time and store that water in their body.

A camel that is 1 thousand pounds can drink as much as 250 pounds of water at one time.

The feet of camels are very wide and flat, so these feet don't sink in the sand.

Some people ride camels the way we ride horses, and people even have camel races.

C

The Camel and the Pig

Is it better to be tall or better to be short? A pig and a camel did not agree. The camel said, "It is easy to see that it is better to be tall."

"No, that is not true," the pig said. "It is far better to be short than to be tall."

Soon, the camel and the pig were yelling at each other. "It's better to be tall," the camel shouted.

"No way," the pig shouted. "Short is better, better, better."

At last a cow became tired of all this shouting and yelling. She said to the camel, "If tall is better, you should be able to show us why it is better." Then she said to the pig, "If short is better, you should be able to show us why it is better." ✦ Then the cow said, "If you do not win, you must give something to the one who wins."

The camel said, "I am so sure that I am right, I will give the pig my hump if I do not win."

The pig said, "And I am so sure I am right, I will give up my nose and my tail."

So the camel and the pig went out to see who was right. They came to a garden with a fence around it. Inside were good things to eat.

The camel said, "I am tall. So it is easy for me to reach over the top and eat all I want." And she ate and ate and ate.

The pig did not eat because she could not reach over the fence.

MORE NEXT TIME

Number your paper from 1 through 12.

D INFORMATION ITEMS

1. Camel feet keep camels from sinking in sand. How are camel feet different from pig feet?

    • They are sharper and smaller.

    • They are wider and flatter.

    • They are harder and longer.

2. Are camels used more in **wet places** or **dry places?**

    • wet places   • dry places

3. Camels can go for ▆▆▆ days without drinking water.

4. How many pounds of water can a 1 thousand-pound camel drink at one time? ▆▆▆ pounds.

5. What's the title of this story?

   - The Cow and the Horse

   - How Animals are Different

   - The Camel and the Pig

6. Which animal believed that tall was better?

   - pig   - cow   - camel

7. Which animal believed that short was better?

   - pig   - cow   - camel

8. Which animal got tired of the yelling and shouting?

   - pig   - cow   - camel

9. What did the camel agree to give up if she was not right?

   - feet   - hump   - head

10. What did the pig agree to give up if she was not right?

   - teeth   - nose   - tail

11. Which animal was able to eat at the garden?

    - camel   - pig   - cow

12. Why was she able to eat from the garden?

    - She could open the gate.

    - She could jump over the fence.

    - She could reach over the fence.

END OF LESSON 7

8

A

1
1. writing
2. William
3. apartment
4. construction
5. finger

2
1. anymore
2. touching
3. promised
4. peeking
5. you've
6. fighting

3
1. ugliest
2. pencils
3. without
4. centimeters
5. tadpoles
6. tipped

4
1. cent
2. chances
3. faces
4. races
5. dances

5
1. half
2. eaten
3. both
4. inch
5. promise
6. remove

6
1. cloth
2. erase
3. eraser
4. ink
5. shaft
6. sample

Facts About Centimeters

The story you're going to read tells about centimeters. Here are facts about centimeters:

- Centimeters are used to tell how long things are.
- Inches also tell how long things are. An inch is longer than a centimeter.

Here's an inch:

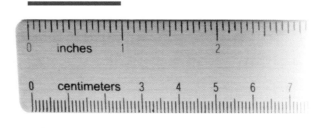

Here's a centimeter.

Hold up your fingers and show your teacher how long an inch is.

Now show your teacher how long a centimeter is.

The Camel and the Pig Trade Parts

The camel had just eaten from a garden. The cow said, "The camel showed that tall is better."

"No," the pig said. "There is another garden down the road. We must go there and I will show you that short is better."

So the camel and the pig and the cow went to the next garden. It had a very high wall, with a hole near the ground. The pig went in the hole and ate good things that were in the garden. The camel didn't eat because the wall was too high.

When the pig came back from the garden, the cow said, "Well, the pig showed that short is better."

"I win," the pig said.

"No, I win," the camel said.

The cow said to the camel, "The pig showed you that short is better. You agreed to give up your hump. So give it up."

Then the cow said to the pig, "The camel showed you that tall is better. You agreed to give up your nose and your tail. So give them to the camel."

The camel and the pig were very sad, but they did what they promised they would do. ✦ The pig got a great big hump. The camel got a pig's nose and a pig's tail.

The pig looked at the camel and said, "You look bad. That nose and tail don't fit you at all. And you look silly without a hump."

The camel said to the pig, "You've got a hump that is bigger than the rest of you."

The cow said, "I will let both of you take back the things you gave up, but you must promise not to yell and fight anymore."

The camel and the pig agreed.

So the camel took back her hump and the pig took back her nose and tail. Then the cow said, "You both look a lot better. And I'm glad that we will not have to hear any more talk about tall and short."

The pig said, "I agree that it is better to be tall some times, but most of the time short is way better than tall."

The camel said, "Not true. Most of the time it's better to be tall than short."

"Oh, no," the cow said and walked away.

THE END

D INFORMATION ITEMS

1. Which is longer, an inch or a centimeter?

   - an inch
   - a centimeter

2. Some of the lines in the box are one inch long. Some of the lines are one centimeter long. **Write the letter of every line that is one inch long.**

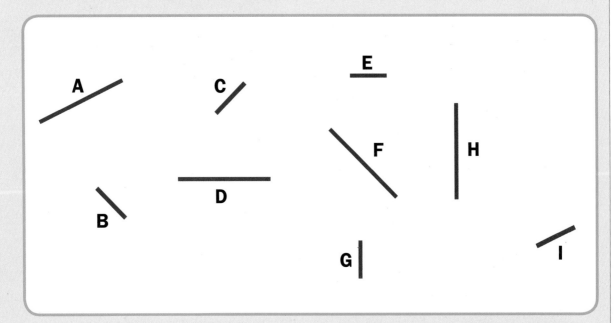

3. Write the letter of every line that is one centimeter long.

E STORY ITEMS

4. What did the camel agree to give up if she was not right?

   - hump
   - feet
   - head

5. What did the pig agree to give up if she was not right?

   • teeth   • tail   • nose

6. Who ate at the first garden?

   • camel   • cow   • pig

7. Who ate at the next garden?

   • camel   • cow   • pig

8. How did the pig get food from this garden?

   • jumped over the wall

   • went through a hole

   • opened the gate

9. Which parts did the pig give to the camel?

   • hump   • nose   • feet   • tail

10. Which part did the camel give to the pig?

    • hump   • nose   • feet   • tail

11. Which animals promised not to talk about tall and short?

    • goat   • cow   • toad   • pig

    • horse   • fish   • dog   • camel

12. Did they keep their promise?

END OF LESSON 8

A

1
1. ruler
2. thought
3. escape
4. writing
5. felt-tipped
6. stream

2
1. dance
2. prance
3. pencil
4. fence

3
1. Mary Williams
2. construction
3. apartment
4. member
5. escaping
6. desk

4
1. basket
2. ink
3. sheet
4. cloth
5. shaft
6. toss

5
1. rod
2. rode
3. cane
4. can
5. wife

6
1. waded
2. eraser
3. boasted
4. holder
5. drills

Felt-Tipped Pens

You'll read a story about a felt-tipped pen. Here are facts about felt-tipped pens:

- Felt-tipped pens have tips that are made of felt. Felt is a kind of cloth.

- The shaft of the pen is filled with ink. The shaft is the long part of the pen that you hold when you write.

- The ink flows down to the tip. Ink is wet. The tip is made of cloth. So when ink gets on the tip, the tip gets wet with ink.

- Most felt-tipped pens do not have an eraser. Ink is not easy to erase. What kind of writing tool does have an eraser?

Joe Williams Wants a New Job

Joe Williams was a felt-tipped pen. He had a wide tip and his color was bright red. Joe's job was construction. He worked with other members of the construction team—pencils, paints, other pens, brushes, and erasers. Their construction job was to make pictures.

All day long, Joe worked with others. They worked very fast. First, Joe would be sitting next to the other pens. Then somebody would pick him up, make a few marks with him, and toss him back with the other pens.

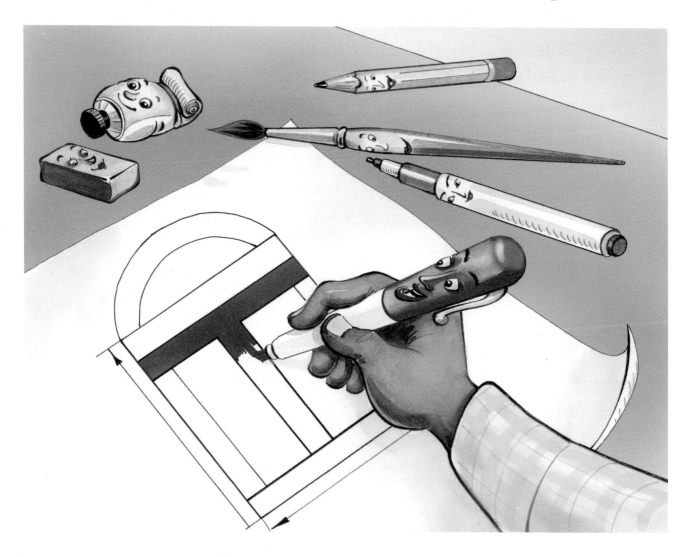

The work was hard, and everybody on the construction team was glad when it was time for lunch. The members of the team would sit and talk about the picture they were making. Then, at one o'clock, work would start again, and it would keep going until the end of the day.

After the work was done, Joe would go to his apartment. ✦ He lived in the desk with his wife, Mary, who worked as a number-one pencil.

Every day, the same thing happened. Joe worked on construction, laying down red lines and red marks. Then he went home. One day, Joe said to himself, "I'm tired of being a felt-tipped pen. I'm tired of laying down red lines. I want a new job."

✿ When Joe told his wife that he was thinking of taking up a new job, she said, "Don't be silly, Joe. What else can you do?" Joe looked at himself. He couldn't work as an eraser because he didn't have an eraser. He couldn't work as a pencil holder, because he didn't have the right shape. He couldn't work as a sheet of paper.

He said to himself, "Let's face it, Joe. You're just made to be a red felt-tipped pen." Then he said, "But I must be able to do something else."

Joe felt sad, but he didn't stop ✿ thinking about a new job.

MORE NEXT TIME

Number your paper from 1 through 14.

D INFORMATION ITEMS

1. Most felt-tipped pens do not have an eraser because ink is �█▍ .

   • wet   • hard to erase   • red

2. Which letter shows the ink?

3. Which letter shows the shaft?

4. Which letter shows the felt tip?

5. The pen in the picture does not have an eraser. Write the letter that shows where an eraser would go on the pen.

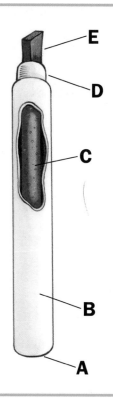

E. STORY ITEMS

6. What color ink did Joe Williams have?

7. What kind of tip did Joe Williams have?

8. What kind of job did Joe have?

   - making red lines
   - making blue lines
   - making erasers

9. Write the names of 3 other members of the construction team.

   - cans
   - erasers
   - pencils
   - brushes
   - drills
   - baskets

10. Where did Joe live?

11. His wife was named ▩ .

12. Did she think that Joe could get a new job?

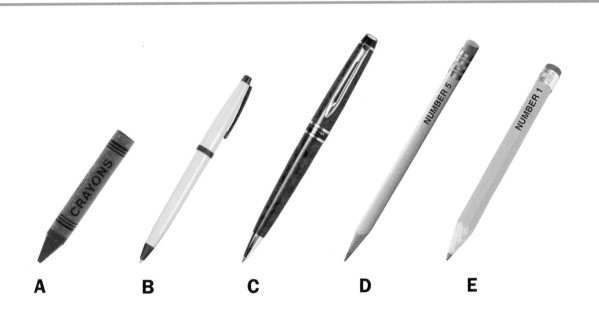

A   B   C   D   E

13. One of the things in the picture could be Joe's wife.
Write the letter of the object that could be Joe's wife.

14. Object D could not be Joe's wife because Joe's wife is ▩ .

A

1
1. hairstyle
2. broccoli
3. sentence
4. message
5. tomorrow
6. regular

2
1. adult
2. correct
3. actually
4. change
5. question
6. students

3
1. brain
2. brainless
3. begin
4. beginning
5. bathroom

4
1. bald
2. Stephanie
3. whatever
4. desks
5. noses
6. shaved

5
1. changing
2. adults
3. copy
4. copied
5. copycats

6
1. ponytail
2. wear
3. above
4. mistake

Stephanie's Ponytail

A story by Robert Munsch
Art by Michael Martchenko

One day Stephanie went to her mom and said, "None of the kids in my class have a ponytail. I want a nice ponytail coming right out the back."

So Stephanie's mom gave her a nice ponytail coming right out the back.

When Stephanie went to school, the other kids looked at her and said, "Ugly, ugly, *very* ugly."

Stephanie said, "It's *my ponytail* and *I* like it."

The next morning, when Stephanie went to school, all the other girls had ponytails coming out the back.

Stephanie looked at them and said, "You are all a bunch of copycats. You just do whatever I do. You don't have a brain in your heads."

The next morning the mom said, "Stephanie, would you like a ponytail coming out the back?"

Stephanie said, "No."

"Then that's that," said her mom. "That's the only place you can do ponytails."

"No, it's not," said Stephanie. "I want one coming out the side, just above my ear."

"Very strange," said the mom. "Are you sure that is what you want?"

"Yes," said Stephanie.

So her mom gave Stephanie a nice ponytail coming out right above her ear.

When she went to school, the other kids saw her and said, "Ugly, ugly, *very* ugly." Stephanie said, "It's *my ponytail* and *I* like it."

The next morning, when Stephanie came to school, all the girls, and even some of the boys, had nice ponytails coming out just above their ears.

The next morning the mom said, "Stephanie, would you like a ponytail coming out the back?"

Stephanie said, "NNNO."

"Would you like one coming out the side?"

"NNNO!"

"Then that's that," said her mom. "There is no other place you can do ponytails."

"Yes, there is," said Stephanie. "I want one coming out the top of my head like a tree."

"That's very, very strange," said her mom. "Are you sure that is what you want?"

"Yes," said Stephanie.

So her mom gave Stephanie a nice ponytail coming out the top of her head like a tree. When Stephanie went to school, the other kids saw her and said, "Ugly, ugly, *very* ugly."

Stephanie said, "It's *my ponytail* and *I* like it."

The next day all of the girls and all of the boys had ponytails coming out the top. It looked like broccoli was growing out of their heads.

The next morning Stephanie said, "Everybody will copy me! I don't want a ponytail."

"Wait!" said Stephanie's mom. "I do not think they will copy THIS ponytail."

Then, Stephanie's mom made a ponytail that went down right in front of Stephanie's NOSE.

When Stephanie went to school all the kids yelled, "Ugly, ugly, *very* ugly."

"I do not care what you think," said Stephanie. "It's *my* ponytail and *I* like it."

The next day all of the girls and all of the boys, and even the teacher, had ponytails coming out the front and hanging down in front of their noses. None of them could see where they were going. They bumped into the desks and they bumped into each other. They bumped into the walls, and, by mistake, three girls went into the boys' bathroom.

Stephanie yelled, "You are a bunch of brainless copycats. You just do whatever I do. When I come tomorrow I am going to have . . . SHAVED MY HEAD!"

The first person to come the next day was the teacher. She had shaved her head and she was bald.

The next to come were the boys. They had shaved their heads and they were bald.

The next to come were the girls. They had shaved their heads and they were bald.

The last person to come was Stephanie, and she had . . .

a nice little ponytail coming right out the back.

A

1

1. circus
2. famous
3. human
4. blood
5. expensive
6. thousand
7. might

2

1. Martha Jumpjump
2. Henry Ouch
3. Aunt Fanny
4. Carl Goodscratch

3

1. bread
2. world
3. flea
4. fame
5. insect
6. boasted
7. object

4

1. learn
2. taught
3. complete
4. round
5. ruler
6. hogged

5

1. ride
2. rid
3. her
4. here
5. pin
6. pine

6

1. dancing
2. danced
3. slowest
4. removed
5. escaping
6. sentences
7. thoughts

Centimeters

The story you'll read today tells about centimeters. Remember, **a centimeter is shorter than an inch.**

Every line in this row is one centimeter long:

Every line in this row is one inch long:

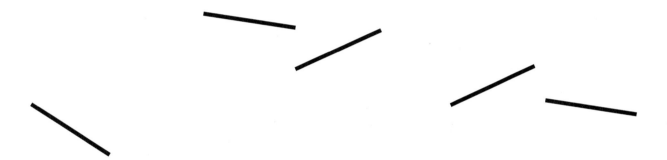

Joe Williams Gets a New Job

Every night, Joe went home and thought about jobs that he might do, but he didn't come up with any good thoughts. Then one night, Joe had a good thought. He was watching his wife, Mary. She was singing to herself, and she was dancing. When a number-one pencil dances, she makes a little line on the floor. Then she jumps and makes another little line right next to the first line. As Joe watched her make these lines, he jumped up from the chair and jumped across the floor. "I've got it," he yelled. "I've got it!"

Mary stopped dancing and looked at Joe. "What are you thinking?"

Joe got down on the floor and said, "I want you to make marks on me. Make marks that are one centimeter apart. Make marks all down the side of my shaft. If I have those marks on my shaft, I can work as a ruler. ★

Mary said, "Maybe that will work. Let's see."

She made the marks on Joe's side. Then she made numbers by the marks. When she was done, Joe jumped up and looked at himself. "Wow, that's nice," he said. He kept turning around and looking at himself. "I'll be the only round ruler on the construction team."

The next day, Joe didn't line up with the other pens. He went over with the rulers.

One ruler said, "What do you think you're doing here, pen?"

"I'm now a ruler," Joe said.

Another ruler said, "We'll soon find out if you're really a ruler. It's just about time to work."

Pretty soon, somebody picked up Joe and said, "Let's see how this round ruler works." The person used Joe as a ruler. "This round ruler works very well," the person said. And from that day on, Joe had a new job. He was a round ruler. And he was happy.

THE END

Number your paper from 1 through 16.

D STORY ITEMS

1. One of the things in the picture could be Joe's wife. Write the letter of the object that could be Joe's wife.

2. Object B could not be Joe's wife because Joe's wife is ▇ .

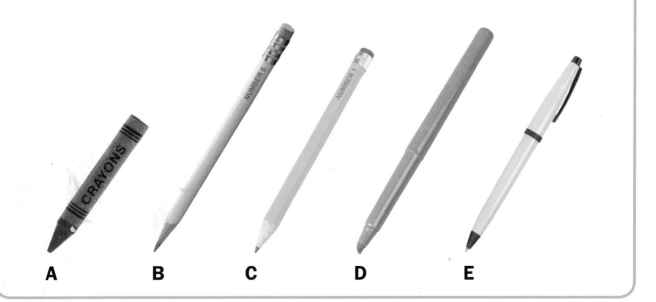

A   B   C   D   E

Here's the rule:

The faster Mary dances, the shorter her lines.

3. Write the letter of the lines Mary made when she danced the fastest.

4. Write the letter of the lines Mary made when she danced the slowest.

A	B	C	D	E

E SKILL ITEMS

Use the words in the box to write complete sentences.

remove	weight	sing	waded
measure	tadpoles	pounds	circus

5. They ▨▨ into the stream to ▨▨ ▨▨ .

6. You ▨▨ your ▨▨ in ▨▨ .

7. Which has a tall straight trunk, an apple tree or forest tree?

   • apple tree   • forest tree

8. Which has smaller branches, an apple tree or forest tree?

   • apple tree   • forest tree

9. A forest fire may burn for ▇▇▇ .

   • seasons   • years   • weeks

10. A forest fire kills both ▇▇▇ and ▇▇▇ .

    • plants   • whales   • fish   • animals

11. About how many years could it take for the forest to grow back?

    • 20 years   • 200 years   • 100 years

12. Camel feet keep camels from sinking in sand. How are camel feet different from pig feet?

    • They are harder and longer.

    • They are sharper and smaller.

    • They are wider and flatter.

For items 13 through 16, read each thing that Tina did. Then write the season that tells when she did it.

- summer
- fall
- spring
- winter

13. Made leaves and white flowers

14. Went to sleep

15. Made big red apples

16. Made little apples where each flower was

END OF LESSON 11

A

1

1. Russia
2. great
3. surprise
4. tomorrow
5. probably
6. treating
7. learning

2

1. Aunt Fanny
2. Carl Goodscratch
3. Henry Ouch
4. Martha Jumpjump

3

1. second
2. minute
3. hour
4. week

4

1. French
2. juggle
3. ladies
4. circus
5. famous
6. cage
7. trained

5

1. blood
2. bread
3. human
4. flea
5. world
6. bunnies
7. turkey

6

1. New York
2. thousands
3. gentlemen
4. expensive
5. insect
6. hogged
7. Harry

Facts About Fleas

You'll read about fleas in today's story. Here are some facts about fleas:

- Fleas are insects.
  All insects have six legs.
  So fleas have six legs.
- Fleas bite and suck blood.
- A row of about five big fleas is one centimeter long.
- Different kinds of fleas live on different kinds of animals.

Cat fleas like to live on cats. Cat fleas are different from dog fleas. Dog fleas are different from human fleas. Human fleas are different from rat fleas.

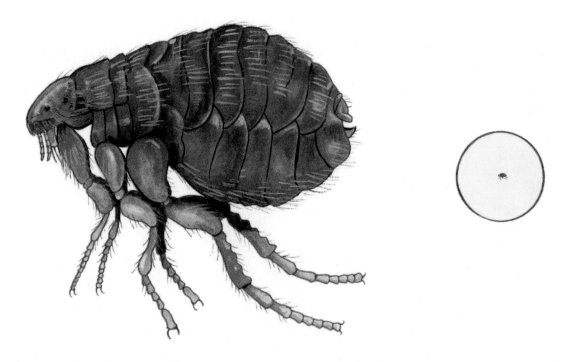

The pictures show a dog flea.

Aunt Fanny's Flea Circus

Aunt Fanny's Flea Circus was formed in 1993. The circus had a great line-up of acts. Aunt Fanny had the most famous fleas in the world. One act was Carl Goodscratch, who dove 48 centimeters into two drops of water.

When Carl did his dive, the people watching the show would sit without making a sound. Then they would cheer and stamp their feet. Another act that crowds loved was Martha Jumpjump, who skipped rope on a high wire. (The high wire was really a spider web that had been fixed up so that Martha wouldn't stick to it.)

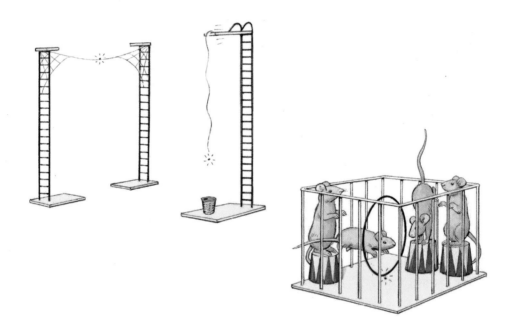

Then there was the French flea, Henry Ouch, the flea who trained rats. He would get into a cage with four or five rats and have them do all kinds of tricks. If they did not do what he told them to do, he would jump on their backs and bite them.

Aunt Fanny's Flea Circus went around the world, bringing in big crowds and making lots of money. ★ But in 1999, Aunt Fanny and the fleas started to fight a lot.

The fleas said that Aunt Fanny was hogging all the fame. Aunt Fanny said that she could do what she wanted because she owned the circus. The fleas were mad at Fanny because of the way she acted. After each show, people would come up to Fanny. "Great show, Fanny," they would say. The only thing Fanny did in the show was wave a stick at the fleas. The fleas did the real work.

Also, Aunt Fanny hogged all the money. She kept the poor fleas locked in a little box while she lived in an expensive apartment. She fed the fleas dry bread while she ate expensive food. She put thousands of dollars into the bank, but she didn't give the fleas a dime.

One night the fleas made up their minds that things had to change.

"She's treating us like dirt," Carl said. "Are we going to take that?"

"No," all the other fleas agreed. "Things must change."

MORE NEXT TIME

D REVIEW ITEMS

1. What do all living things need?

2. What do all living things make?

3. Do all living things grow?

4. Which letter shows where the ground gets warm first?

5. Which letter shows where the ground gets warm last?

The pictures show the same twig in 4 seasons. Write the name of the season for each twig.

6. ▬▬▬▬▬   7. ▬▬▬▬▬   8. ▬▬▬▬▬   9. ▬▬▬▬▬

10. In the fall, are the leaves on trees dead or alive?

11. Camels can go for ▬▬▬ days without drinking water.

12. How many pounds of water can a 1 thousand-pound camel drink at one time?

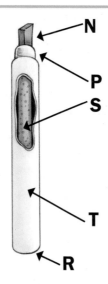

13. Which letter shows the felt tip?

14. Which letter shows the ink?

15. Which letter shows the shaft?

16. Write the letter that shows where an eraser would go on a pen.

END OF LESSON 12

A

1

1. meter
2. yea
3. directions
4. Russia
5. passage

2

1. greatest
2. minute
3. fancy
4. middle
5. surprise
6. skipping

3

1. propped
2. second
3. tomorrow
4. money
5. scared
6. packed

4

1. week
2. ladies
3. cage
4. hour
5. hoop
6. taught

5

1. probably
2. turkey
3. gentlemen
4. juggle
5. steel
6. learning

6

1. men
2. mean
3. hope
4. hop
5. bit
6. bite

B Passage 1

Learning About Time

Names that tell about time tell how long it takes for something to happen. A **week** tells about time. A week is seven days long. So if something will happen a week from now, it will happen seven days from now.

An **hour** is another name that tells about time. If you spent an hour watching TV, you may be able to watch two shows.

A **second** is a name that tells about time. When you count slowly, each number takes about one second.

A **minute** is a name that tells about time. A minute is much smaller than an hour.

Remember, names that tell about time tell how long it takes for something to happen.

Facts About Flea Circuses

When we left Aunt Fanny in the last story, the fleas were mad at her. Name three things they were mad about.

The fleas in the story talk, so we know they are make-believe fleas. But there are such things as flea circuses. And these flea circuses do have fleas that put on acts.

Here are some facts about real flea circuses:

- Most fleas that are used in flea circuses come from Russia.
- Fleas have been taught to juggle things.
- Fleas have been taught to jump through hoops.
- Some fleas have been taught to pull things that weigh a hundred times more than a flea.
- The first trick a flea must be taught is to walk instead of hop. Fleas like to take a great hop to go from place to place. But they can walk.

After they have been taught to walk, they can be taught to walk on a high wire or to pull a cart.

The Fleas Surprise Aunt Fanny

The fleas in Aunt Fanny's Flea Circus were tired of the way Aunt Fanny was treating them. They made up their minds to do something about it. Carl spoke for all the fleas. He went to Aunt Fanny and tried to tell her that she would have to change her ways. But she wouldn't even listen to him.

"Please, Carl," she said. "Can't you see I'm late for dinner? Now be a good little flea and go back to your nice little box."

"Go to your dinner," he yelled as loud as he could. "Things will be different tomorrow."

Aunt Fanny was in for a great big surprise the next day. The circus was packed with people. Aunt Fanny picked up her stick and people clapped. "Ladies and gentlemen," she said. "You will see the greatest flea show in the world. The first act is the famous Martha Jumpjump skipping rope on the high wire." Aunt Fanny waved her stick, and Martha went up to the high wire. But she didn't skip rope. She walked to the middle of the wire and fell off. "Booo," the crowd yelled.

The next act was Henry Ouch. He got in the cage with three rats. But he didn't make the rats do tricks. He hopped around the cage while the rats went to sleep. "Boooo," the crowd yelled.

MORE NEXT TIME

Number your paper from 1 through 12.

SKILL ITEMS

Here are titles for different stories:

a. 100 Ways to Cook Turkey

b. Why Smoking Will Hurt You

c. A Funny Story

1. One story tells about reading something that makes you laugh. Write the letter of that title.

2. One story tells about something that is bad for you. Write the letter of that title.

3. One story tells about how to make different meals out of one thing. Write the letter of that title.

Here's a rule: **All the people got mad and yelled.**

4. Tim is a person. So what else do you know about Tim?

5. Liz is a person. So what else do you know about Liz?

The fly boasted about escaping from the spider.

6. What word tells about getting away from something?

7. What word means **bragged?**

F REVIEW ITEMS

8. Which is longer, a centimeter or an inch?

9. How many legs does an insect have?

10. How many legs does a spider have?

11. How many legs does a flea have?

12. If a beetle is an insect, what else do you know about a beetle?

END OF LESSON 13

A

1

1. scared
2. usually
3. fancy
4. disappear
5. group
6. refer

2

1. crowd
2. south
3. measure
4. money
5. given
6. treat

3

1. pillow
2. north
3. meter
4. yea
5. loop
6. paid

4

1. covering
2. propped
3. steel
4. directions
5. seven

5

1. made
2. mad
3. sleep
4. slept
5. robe
6. rob

Meters

You're going to read about meters. We use meters to measure how long things are.

A meter is 100 centimeters long.

Directions on a Map

You are going to read about 4 directions: **north, south, east,** and **west.**

Maps always show:

> north on the top.
>
> south on the bottom.
>
> east on this side: $\longrightarrow$
>
> west on this side: $\longleftarrow$

If something on a map goes north, it goes this way: $\uparrow$

If something on a map goes south, it goes this way: $\downarrow$

If something on a map goes this way $\longrightarrow$ which direction is it going?

If something on a map goes this way $\longleftarrow$ which direction is it going?

Aunt Fanny Changes Her Ways

The fleas had given Aunt Fanny a surprise. Martha Jumpjump did not do her act. Henry Ouch did not do his act. The crowd did not like the show at all, and Aunt Fanny was getting scared. If the rest of the fleas did not do their acts, Aunt Fanny would have to give money back to the people who paid to see the show.

The next act was Carl Goodscratch. He went up to the top of his 48 centimeter ladder. Then he looked up at Aunt Fanny and said, "Don't you think that you should treat us better? Don't you think that you should give us more money and give us a better place to live?"

Aunt Fanny looked at the little flea. Then she looked at the crowd. They looked mad. "Yes, Carl, yes, yes, yes," she said. ✦ "Do the dive and I will share everything with you."

"Do you really mean that?" Carl asked.

"Yes, yes, yes, yes, yes," Aunt Fanny said. Her hand was shaking so much that the stick was making a wind.

✿ So Carl did a dive. People say it was the best dive he ever did. He turned around five times. He made seven loops. And he landed in the water without making any splash at all.

The crowd went wild. "Yea, yea," the people cheered. "What a show!" they shouted.

Now everybody in Aunt Fanny's Flea Circus is happy. Aunt Fanny is happy because the fleas work harder and put on a better show. The fleas are happy because they live in a great big fancy dog house that is a meter high and a meter wide. And they have ✿ lots and lots of money.

THE END

Number your paper from 1 through 14.

Here are titles for different stories:

A. Jane Goes on a Train   C. My Dog Likes Cats

B. The Hot Summer   D. The Best Meal

1. One story tells about eating good food. Write the letter of that title.

2. One story tells about somebody taking a trip. Write the letter of that title.

3. One story tells about a time of year when people go swimming a lot. Write the letter of that title.

4. One story tells about pets. Write the letter of that title.

Use the words in the box to write complete sentences.

escaping		learning	visited	remove
smooth	first	waded	tadpoles	boasted

5. They ____ into the stream to ____ ____ .
6. The fly ____ about ____ from the spider.

F REVIEW ITEMS

7. In the spring, are the leaves on trees **dead** or **alive?**
8. Are those leaves **wet** or **dry?**

9. How many legs does an insect have?
10. How many legs does a spider have?
11. If a bee is an insect, what else do you know about a bee?
12. Where do the fleas in flea circuses usually come from?
13. What's the first thing that fleas must be taught?
14. Write the 4 names that tell about time.
    - centimeter
    - hour
    - inch
    - minute
    - week
    - second
    - meter

END OF LESSON 14

A

1

1. Alaska
2. escape
3. rough
4. favorite
5. opposite
6. support
7. decide

2

1. full-grown
2. tadpoles
3. sometimes
4. goldfish

3

1. boast
2. Goad
3. toaster
4. floating

4

1. members
2. pillow
3. hunters
4. robin
5. covered

5

1. metal
2. family
3. chasing
4. strong
5. disappears
6. refer
7. group

6

1. shore
2. catch
3. rich
4. circus
5. hound
6. front
7. shoot

Facts About Toads and Frogs

Toads and frogs are members of the same family. Here are facts about toads and frogs:

- They are born in water, and they live in the water until they are full-grown. Then they move onto the land.

- At first toads and frogs are tadpoles that have no legs.

- Then the tadpoles grow two back legs.

- Then they grow two front legs.

- The body gets bigger and the tail disappears. Now they are full-grown toads or frogs.

- Now that their legs are big and strong, frogs and toads live on the land.

Remember, they are born in the water and grow up in the water. Then they move to the land.

c

Goad the Toad

Once there was a toad named Goad. Goad was the biggest toad you have ever seen. Goad was bigger than a baseball. She was even bigger than a toaster.

Goad was not only big. She was smart. She was smarter than a trained seal. Not only was Goad big and smart, Goad was fast. She was faster than a cat chasing a mouse.

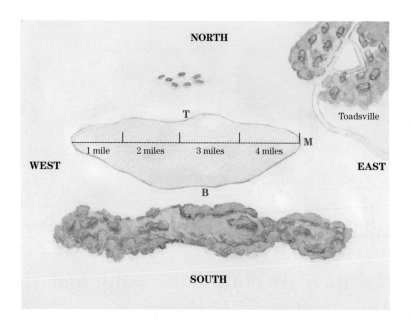

Goad lived near a large lake called Four Mile Lake. It was four miles from one end of the lake to the other.

Goad liked to visit places on Four Mile Lake. Sometimes, she would hop over to the logs near the north shore of the lake. Sometimes, she would hop over the hills on the south shore. Sometimes, she would go for a swim near the east shore of the lake.

When Goad was in the water, she was not fast. She could not swim as fast as a seal or a goldfish. In fact, she could not swim as fast as a very slow frog. When Goad was in the water, she looked like a floating pillow with two big eyes.

Because Goad was so big, and so fast, and so smart, thousands of hunters went to Four Mile Lake every year to see if they could catch Goad. People from the circus knew that if they had Goad, they could put on a show that would bring thousands of people to the circus. Hunters from zoos knew that people would come from all over to visit any zoo that had a toad like Goad. Some hunters came because they wanted to become rich. But nobody was able to catch Goad.

MORE NEXT TIME

D SKILL ITEMS

Rule: **Frogs have smooth skin.**

1. The rule tells something about any ▓▓▓ .

Rule: **Birds have two feet.**

2. The rule tells something about any ▓▓▓ .

3. Is a robin a bird?

4. Does the rule tell about a robin?

5. Does the rule tell about an ape?

Rule: **The biggest mountains were covered with snow.**

6. What's the only thing that rule tells about?

  • any mountain

  • the biggest mountains

  • any frog

7. Does the rule tell about Happy Valley?

8. Write the letter of each picture the rule tells about.

A   B   C   D

Here are titles for different stories:

a. Liz Goes to the Zoo   b. A Pretty New Hat

c. The Green Dog

9. One story tells about someone who went to look at animals. Write the letter of that title.

10. One story tells about a funny-looking animal. Write the letter of that title.

11. One story tells about something you put on your head. Write the letter of that title.

E   REVIEW ITEMS

12. Which is longer, a centimeter or an inch?

13. Some of the lines in the box are one inch long. Some of the lines are one centimeter long. Write the letter of every line that is one inch long.

14. Write the letter of every line that is one centimeter long.

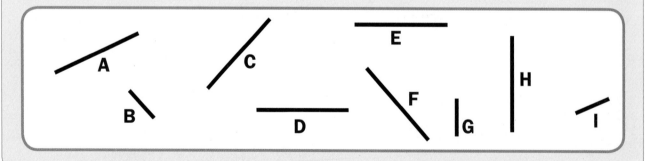

15. Where do the fleas in flea circuses usually come from?

16. What's the first thing that fleas must be taught?

END OF LESSON 15

A

1
1. covered
2. visited
3. escaped
4. noticed
5. removed
6. stationed
7. underlined

2
1. metal
2. favorite
3. evening
4. Toadsville
5. hundreds
6. outline

3
1. warts
2. belly
3. Alaska
4. first
5. opposite
6. supporting
7. rushed

4
1. gone
2. shovels
3. tongue
4. rough
5. there
6. underground
7. deer

5
1. feel
2. felt
3. cap
4. cape
5. bet
6. beat

More Facts About Toads and Frogs

Toads and frogs are members of the same family. But toads are different from frogs. Here are some facts about how toads and frogs are different:

- Toads have skin that is rough and covered with warts.
- No toads have teeth, but some frogs have teeth.
- The back legs of toads are not as big or strong as the back legs of frogs.

Goad Uses Her First Trick

Goad lived near Four Mile Lake. Down the road from the lake was a town. The name of that town was Toadsville. It was named Toadsville because so many people who visited the town had come to hunt for a big, smart, fast toad. And in the evening you could find hundreds of people sitting around Toadsville talking about Goad. First they would talk about some of the traps that had been made to catch Goad. Then they would tell how Goad escaped. One of their favorite stories is the one of the great big net.

Five hunters from Alaska had come to Four Mile Lake with a net that was nearly a mile wide. They waited until Goad was on a hill where there were no trees, just some white rocks. ★ Then they flew over the hill in a plane and dropped the great big net over the hill. Goad was under the net. The five hunters rushed to the place where Goad had last been seen. But there was no Goad. There was some grass and five large white rocks.

The hunters removed the net and began to go over every centimeter of the ground.

Suddenly, one of the hunters noticed that the biggest rock was moving. The biggest rock wasn't a rock at all. It was Goad.

She had moved near the other rocks. Then she had turned over on her back so that her white belly was showing. That belly looked like a white rock. Suddenly she turned over. "There she is," one of the hunters yelled, but before the others could turn around, Goad hopped down the side of the hill and was gone.

MORE NEXT TIME

D **SKILL ITEMS**

Write the word from the box that means the same thing as the underlined part of each sentence.

weight	measure	leaves	sometimes
grove	family	usually	evening

1. The deer ran into the <u>small group of trees</u> to hide.

2. <u>Most of the time</u> she goes home after school.

3. She used a ruler to <u>see</u> how long the rope was.

4. Look at object A, object B, and object C. Write at least **2** ways all 3 objects are the same.

Object A   **Object B**   **Object C**

- They are all big.
- They are pink.
- They are not round.
- They are striped.
- They are circles.

The workers propped up the cage with steel bars.

5. What **2** words refer to supporting something?

6. What word names a strong metal?

7. What objects were made of a strong metal?

8. What object was propped up?

---

9. Which is longer, one inch or one centimeter?

10. Some of the lines in the box are one inch long. Some of the lines are one centimeter long. Write the letter of every line that is one centimeter long.

11. Write the letter of every line that is one inch long.

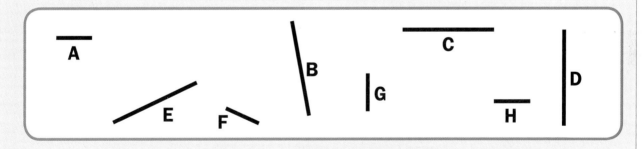

12. What color are the flowers that apple trees make?

13. When do those flowers come out?

14. What grows in each place where there was a flower?

17

A

1

1. famous
2. women
3. breath
4. tongue
5. England
6. silence

2

1. stubby
2. family
3. belly
4. sticky
5. already
6. sixty

3

1. shovels
2. seconds
3. wooden
4. underground
5. halfway
6. catching
7. doghouse

4

1. length
2. blue
3. hundred
4. noticed
5. evening

5

1. distance
2. balloon
3. swallow
4. fourth

How Far Apart Things Are

Names that tell about length or distance tell how far apart things are. Aunt Fanny bought a fancy doghouse that was one meter tall and one meter wide. A ruler is one foot long.

A **mile** is a name that tells how far apart things are. If two things are a mile apart, they are more than 5 thousand feet apart.

A **meter** is a name that tells about length.

A **centimeter** is a name that tells about length.

Remember, miles, feet, meters, centimeters, and inches are names that tell about length. They tell how far apart things are.

How Toads Catch Flies

Toads eat flies. A toad catches flies with its long, long tongue. A toad's tongue is almost as long as the toad.

A toad's tongue is covered with sticky goo. The tongue moves so fast that it hits a fly before the fly can move. The fly sticks to the tongue.

When the toad pulls its tongue back, the fly comes with it. The pictures below show a toad's tongue catching a fly.

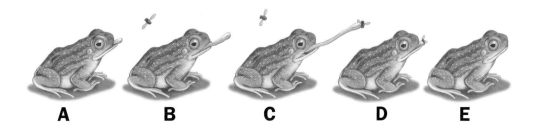

A   **B**   **C**   **D**   **E**

Food Traps

The people in Toadsville like to tell stories about Goad and how she escaped from traps. They tell about how she once escaped from the great big net. The people also tell how Goad got away from food traps. One of the hunters' favorite tricks was to make food traps.

All food traps work the same way. You put out some food that a toad likes. Maybe you put some blue flies on the ground. My, my, how toads love those blue flies. Then you make a trap that closes on the toad when it goes for the food.

PICTURE 1

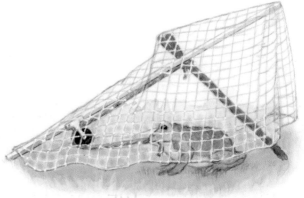

PICTURE 2

PICTURE 3

If the pole tips over, the toad is trapped in the net. Hunters put blue flies at the end of the string. When the toad eats the flies, the string moves and the pole falls over. ✦

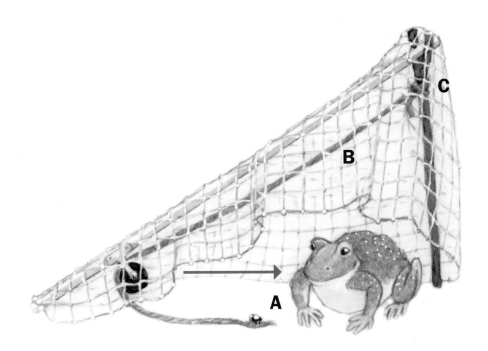

PICTURE 4

Remember, a fly is on the end of the string. So when the fly moves, the string moves. And when the string moves, the pole moves. That pole holds up a net. So when the fly moves, the string moves. And when the string moves, the pole moves. And when the pole moves, the net falls over the toad.

If you believe the stories they tell in the town of Toadsville, Goad has escaped from over five hundred food traps. Not all these stories are true. Goad has really escaped from four hundred food traps, but that's a lot of escaping for one toad. How did she do it? You already know one of her tricks. You'll find out about more of her tricks in the next story.

E **SKILL ITEMS**

Rule: **Dogs have four legs.**

1. Write the letter of each object the rule tells about.

A B C

D E F

Write the word or words from the box that mean the same thing as the underlined part of each sentence.

| danger | thousand | a meter | half | bark |
| great | during | ruler | measure | an inch |

2. The <u>tree's covering</u> was full of holes.

3. She went on a <u>wonderful</u> trip.

4. The string was <u>100 centimeters</u> long.

Here are titles for different stories:

a. The Hungry Frog   b. The Fly That Couldn't Fly

c. How to Grow Roses

5. One story tells about an insect that was different. Write the letter of that title.

6. One story tells about an animal that wanted some food. Write the letter of that title.

7. One story tells about pretty plants. Write the letter of that title.

Use the words in the box to complete the sentences.

steel	third	down	boasted	point
propped	howled	escaping	up	

8. The fly ▆▆ about ▆▆ from the spider.
9. The workers ▆▆ ▆▆ the cage with ▆▆ bars.

F STORY ITEM

10. People in Toadsville said that Goad had escaped from over five hundred food traps. But Goad had really escaped from ▆▆ food traps.

11. Some things happen as tadpoles grow. Write the letter that tells what happens first.

    a. They grow back legs   c. Their tail disappears.

    b. They turn blue.   d. They grow front legs.

12. Write the letter that tells what happens last.

13. Write the letter of each toad in the picture.

For items 14 through 17, read each thing that Tina did. Then write the season that tells when she did it.

   • winter   • spring   • summer   • fall

14. Made little apples where each flower was

15. Went to sleep

16. Made big red apples

17. Made leaves and white flowers

END OF LESSON 17

A

1

1. decide
2. group
3. binoculars
4. instructions
5. learn
6. phrase

2

1. tion
2. sion
3. ar
4. al
5. aw

3

1. propped
2. stationed
3. boasted
4. swallowed
5. decided
6. popped

4

1. steel
2. third
3. sixty
4. breath
5. famous
6. wild

5

1. gulp
2. fourth
3. England
4. blast
5. silence
6. tramping

6

1. size
2. manx
3. type
4. cannot
5. state
6. phrases

Facts About Moles

Today's story tells something about moles. Here are some facts about moles:

- Moles are animals that spend nearly all their time underground.
- There are different types of moles. Some are big. Some have almost no hair.
- Bigger moles are about the same size as toads.
- Moles cannot see very well. Some types of moles cannot see at all. They even have skin growing over their eyes.
- Moles have legs that work like shovels.

The Opposite Direction

You're going to learn about things that move in the opposite direction. If you move north, the opposite direction is south. If you move up, the opposite direction is down. If you move to the left, the opposite direction is to the right.

What's the opposite direction of north?

What's the opposite direction of down?

What's the opposite of east?

Point to the front of the room.

Now point in the opposite direction.

Point to the floor.

Now point in the opposite direction.

D

Goad's Four Tricks

Goad has escaped from four hundred food traps. She has four tricks that she uses to escape from those traps. One trick is to make herself look like a rock, the way she did when she escaped from the great net. Her second trick is to dig. You wouldn't think that a toad the size of a pillow could dig very fast, but you have never seen Goad dig. She can dig so fast that worms get mad at her. She can dig faster than a dog. She can even dig faster than a mole. And moles have legs like shovels.

Goad's third trick is to eat the trap. If the food trap is a big wooden box that drops over Goad, that fat toad just smiles to herself and starts eating.

Her fourth trick is to blow the trap away. That's right. She takes in a big breath of air. When she does this, she gets bigger. She gets so big that she looks just like a brown and green and white balloon. ★ When she is nearly two times the size of a pillow, she blows. The wind comes out of her mouth so fast that she can blow most traps a hundred meters away. That's how she got away from the famous steel trap.

A man came from England. The man boasted that he had made a trap that could hold any toad. "No toad can eat through this trap," he said. "And no toad can dig under this trap if I put it on hard rock."

And that's just what he did. He propped up the steel trap next to the road, where there was no dirt, just hard rock. Then he put sixty blue flies under the trap.

There is no toad in the world that can stay away from sixty blue flies. So before very long, out popped Goad. Her tongue came out. In one gulp, she had swallowed half of the flies. She was ready for her second gulp, when BONG.

MORE NEXT TIME

Number your paper from 1 through 12.

E SKILL ITEMS

Rule: **Tadpoles have a tail.**

1. Jean is a tadpole. So what does the rule tell you about Jean?
   - She has a tail.
   - nothing
2. A cat is not a tadpole. So what does the rule tell you about a cat?
   - It has a tail.
   - nothing
   - It is a tadpole.

Rule: **Cats have eyes.**

3. A robin is not a cat. So what does the rule tell you about a robin?
4. A manx is a cat. So what does the rule tell you about a manx? Complete this sentence: A manx ______ .

5. Look at object **A** and object **B.** Write 3 ways the objects are the same.

Object A **Object B**

(1.) They are both ______ .

(2.) They both have ______ .

(3.) ______ .

Write the word from the box that means the same thing as the underlined part of each sentence.

England	station	famous	steel
breath	bark	Alaska	

6. The <u>tree's covering</u> was burned by the forest fire.

7. This book is <u>well-known</u>.

8. Jill wanted to take a trip to <u>the largest state</u>.

F REVIEW ITEMS

9. Write the letters of the 4 names that tell about length. (Remember, those names tell how far apart things are.)

   a. minute   d. centimeter   g. mile   i. year

   b. hour   e. second   h. meter   j. inch

   c. day   f. week

10. The names in one box tell about time. Write the letter of that box.

11. The names in one box tell about length. Write the letter of that box.

   A | centimeter | inch | meter | mile |

   B | week | year | second | minute | hour |

12. Two things move in opposite directions. One moves toward the front of the room. The other moves toward the ▨ .

END OF LESSON 18

A

1

tion
sion
1. impre<u>ssion</u>
2. sta<u>tion</u>
3. instruc<u>tion</u>
4. ac<u>tion</u>
5. vaca<u>tion</u>
6. men<u>tion</u>

2

1. <u>tramping</u>
2. <u>weakness</u>
3. <u>stubby</u>
4. <u>problem</u>
5. <u>middle</u>
6. <u>leaking</u>

3

1. chance
2. women
3. dreams
4. group
5. wild
6. binoculars

4

1. <u>groups</u>
2. <u>hoped</u>
3. <u>trappers</u>
4. <u>failed</u>
5. <u>decided</u>
6. <u>placed</u>

5

1. wolves
2. holler
3. torch
4. either
5. pair
6. motion

6

1. fifteen
2. arrow
3. erase
4. female
5. baby
6. away

Binoculars

Here is a picture of binoculars:

Follow these instructions:

1. Hold your hands so they make circles.

2. Now look through the circles made by your hands.

Looking through binoculars is like looking through the circles made by your hands. But when you look through binoculars, things look very, very big. Things may look ten times as big as they look through the circles made by your hands.

If you see this through the circles made by your hands,

you would see this through a strong pair of binoculars.

If you saw something that looked one centimeter tall through the circles made by your hands, that thing would look ten centimeters tall through strong binoculars.

How Fast Things Move

Here's the rule: **Names that tell how fast things move have two parts.**

Here's a name that tells how fast things move: **miles per hour.** The two parts are **miles** and **hour.**

Here's another name that tells how fast things move: **meters per second.** The two parts are **meters** and **second.**

Here's a name that does not tell how fast things move: **meters.**

Here's another name that does not tell how fast things move: **hours.**

D

The Brown Family Comes to Catch Goad

The famous steel trap came down over Goad. "I told you I could catch her," the man from England boasted as he ran down the road toward the trap. But before he was halfway there, something happened. You could hear the sound of wind. It sounded like air leaking from a tire. Then there was silence. Then there was a great blast of wind, and the famous steel trap went sailing through the air. Goad had used her fourth trick.

Everybody agreed that steel traps couldn't catch Goad, and nets couldn't hold her either. Hundreds of men, women, boys, and girls came tramping over the hills every summer, but they couldn't catch her. Even trained hunters and trappers failed. But Goad has one weakness, and if you listen to the groups of people talking in the town of Toadsville, you know what her only weakness is. She can't swim fast. When she's in the water, she's like a great fat lump, with stubby legs that can hardly push her along. At least a thousand people must have said, "If we could just find her when she's swimming, there's no way she could get away." ⭐

That sounds like an easy thing to do, but there is one problem. You first have to find Goad when she is in the water.

✿ There's an old man in the town of Toadsville who shows pictures of Goad swimming in the lake. The old man took the pictures from high above the lake. Everyone who sees the pictures says the same sort of thing. They say, "If I saw that toad swimming in the lake like that, I'd get in a boat and catch her."

Sometimes in the summer you can count hundreds of people stationed around the lake, ready for action. Some of the people have binoculars. They sit hour after hour, looking through the binoculars. Their great hope is that they will ✿ see Goad swimming far from the shore of the lake.

Last summer, a group of wild hunters had the chance that everybody dreams about. They spotted Goad swimming in the middle of the lake. And they were ready for action. These wild hunters were part of the famous Brown family. The Brown family was made up of 40 people. Fifteen of them were on vacation at Four Mile Lake, and they decided to spend all their time looking for Goad.

MORE NEXT TIME

Number your paper from 1 through 18.

1. What is Goad's only weakness?

   - She sleeps too much.

   - She has a short tongue.

   - She cannot swim fast.

2. People hoped they could be around when Goad was swimming in the lake because ▮▮▮▮

   - she would be easy to hear.

   - she would be easy to catch.

   - she would be easy to smell.

3. There were 40 people in the Brown family. How many of them were going to try to catch Goad?

   - 39   • 15   • 12

Here are Goad's four tricks for escaping from hunters:
- blow the trap away   • dig
- look like a rock   • eat the trap

4. Goad's first trick was to ▮▮▮▮ .

5. Goad's second trick was to ▮▮▮▮ .

6. Goad's third trick was to ▮▮▮▮ .

7. Goad's fourth trick was to ▮▮▮▮ .

---

8. How did Goad get away from the famous steel trap?

SKILL ITEMS

> Rule: **Trees have leaves.**
>
> 9. An oak is a tree. So what else do you know about an oak?
>
> 10. A bush is not a tree. So what else do you know about a bush?
>
> 11. A weed is not a tree. So what else do you know about a weed?

12. Look at object **A** and object **B.** Write 3 ways the objects are the same.

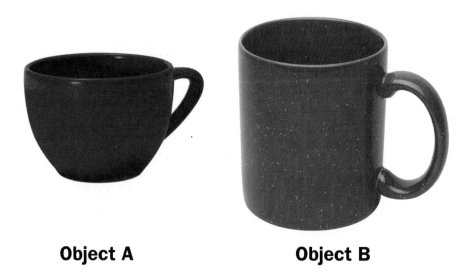

Object A   **Object B**

1. They are both [____] .
2. They both can hold [____] .
3. [____] .

REVIEW ITEMS

13. Which is longer, a centimeter or a meter?

14. How many centimeters long is a meter?

15. Write the letter of each statement that could not be true.

    a. A toad could fly.

    b. A toad could swim.

    c. A toad was as big as a baseball.

    d. A toad was as big as a house.

16. The names in one box tell about time. Write the letter of that box.

17. The names in one box tell about length. Write the letter of that box.

A	centimeter	inch	meter	mile	
B	week	year	second	minute	hour

18. Write the letter of each mole in the picture below.

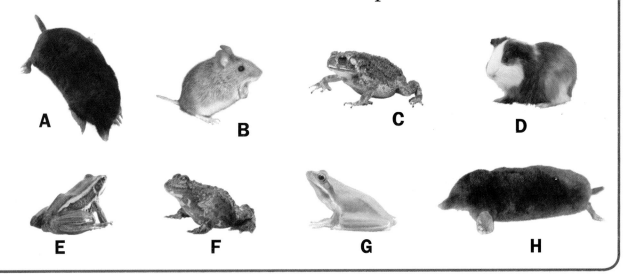

A   B   C   D

E   F   G   H

END OF LESSON 19

A

1

1. emus
2. ostriches
3. illustrate
4. capture
5. passage
6. written
7. buried

2

1. George
2. giraffes
3. quite
4. sign
5. picnic
6. lying

3

1. screaming
2. grounds
3. closed
4. stooping
5. bravest
6. prancing
7. seemed

4

1. allowed
2. excited
3. snapped
4. illustrated
5. crowded
6. growled

5

1. especially
2. cage
3. nowhere
4. elephant
5. wonderful
6. chicken

6

1. barked
2. keeper
3. zookeeper
4. carry
5. carried
6. smelling

GEORGE AT THE ZOO

Written by Sally George
Illustrated by Rob Mancini

George was a small dog who liked large bones and going to picnics. So when his family got out the picnic basket, George got very excited.

"No, George!" said his family. "We're going to the zoo. Dogs can't go to the zoo."

But George liked going in the car, and smelling new smells, and running in new places, and, especially, eating the picnic.

So when his family wasn't looking, George jumped inside the picnic basket. The lid closed, and nobody saw him.

They picked up the picnic basket and carried it out to the car. It was very dark in the picnic basket. And very crowded.

There was more room after George ate the cold chicken, and the ham, and the rolls, and half the cake.

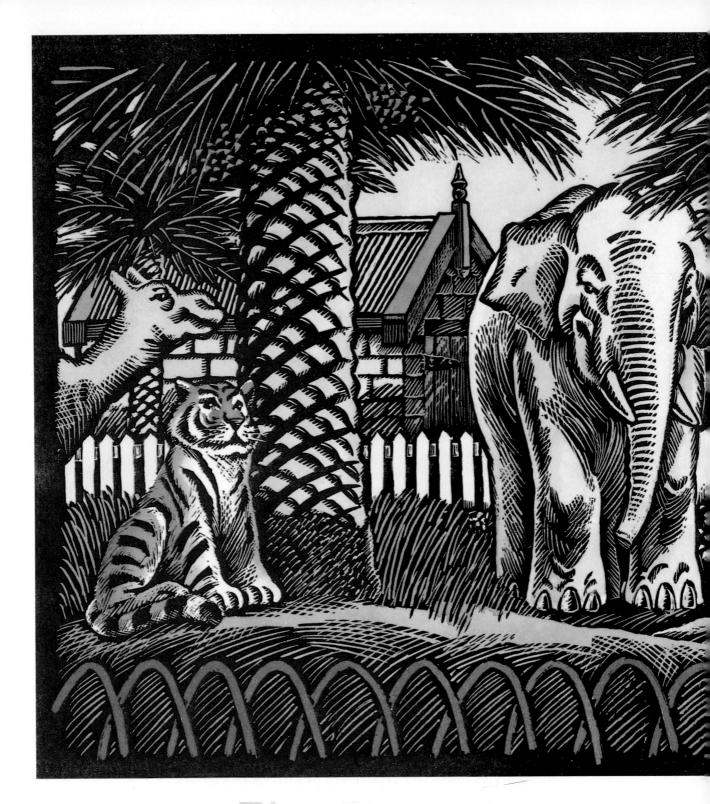

George's family went into the zoo.
"This is a very heavy picnic basket,"
they said. But they didn't open it.
George pushed his nose through the lid.

He smelled lions and tigers, and elephants and camels, and bears and giraffes, and emus and ostriches.

George liked the zoo.

His family walked and walked all over the zoo. Finally, they sat down. They opened the picnic basket.

"Oh, George!" they said. "Bad dog, George!"

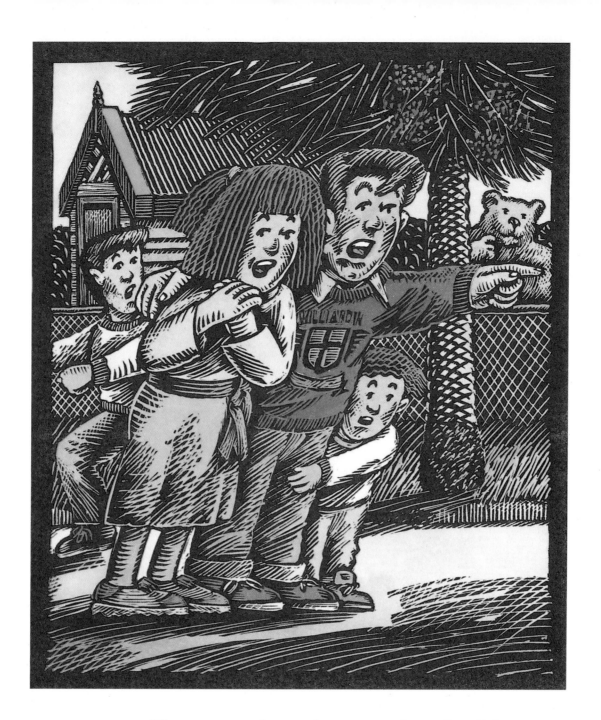

They were just about to shut the lid,
when—men began to shout, women
began to scream, and the children began
to run.

George jumped out of the picnic
basket. There was the biggest cat he
had ever seen. And the cat had the
biggest bone he had ever seen.

George forgot that he had just
eaten the cold chicken, and the ham,
and the rolls, and half the cake.

George wanted that bone!

George's family sat in a tree and called him. But George wanted that bone.

He growled and barked and snapped at the cat. The cat came closer, and roared back the biggest growl that George had ever heard.

George growled and barked and snapped again. The cat stopped, and men came running with trucks and ropes and nets, and chased it into a big cage.

The men locked the cage
with a big lock. The men and
the women and the children
stopped screaming. Everyone
looked at George.

George did not want to be chased
with trucks and ropes and nets and be
locked in a big cage.

He ran back to his picnic basket.

George's family got out of the tree. He knew that they would say, "Bad dog, George!"

But they didn't. They seemed quite happy. They said he was a good dog, a wonderful dog, the bravest, best lion-chasing dog in the whole world.

Then they picked up the picnic
basket and carried it past the sign
that said, "No Dogs Allowed," and
back to the car.

And when they got home, George took the lion's bone out of the picnic basket . . .

and buried it in the garden.

Remember

Written by Pamela Mordecai
Illustrated by Loyal de Neuville

Remember when
the world was tall
and you were small
and legs were all
you saw?

Thin legs
fat legs
dog legs
cat legs.

Table legs
chair legs
dark legs
fair legs.

Quick legs
slow legs
nowhere-
to-go legs.

Jumping legs
prancing legs
skipping legs
dancing legs.

Shoes-and-sock legs
on the rocks legs.

Standing-very-tall legs
running-all-around legs.

Stooping-very-small legs
lying-on-the-ground legs.

Remember when
the world was tall
and you were small
and legs were all
you saw?

A

1

1. toward
2. trouble
3. exactly
4. engine
5. instead
6. month

2

1. impression
2. direction
3. mention
4. question

3

1. motioned
2. stationed
3. interested
4. settled
5. arrived

4

1. holler
2. simple
3. resting
4. torches
5. fourteen
6. we've
7. ordering

5

1. sixteen
2. outsmart
3. grandmother
4. snapshots
5. backward

6

1. wolves
2. great
3. solid
4. twenty
5. enough
6. smoky
7. rush

Animals and Fire

You're going to read about how all wild animals act when there is a fire. Here is the rule: **When there is a fire, all animals try to get away from the fire.**

The animals are not interested in hunting for food. The animals are not interested in fighting with other animals. Deer don't like wolves, but when a fire is near, wolves and deer may run side by side. They do not fight or bother each other.

Smoke and Wind

You're going to read about smoke and wind in today's story. Here's the rule: **The smoke moves in the same direction the wind moves.**

If the wind blows to the north, the smoke moves to the north.

If the wind blows in this direction, ↗, the smoke blows in the same direction, ↗.

Other things that float in the air do the same thing that smoke does. They go in the same direction the wind blows. If the wind blows in this direction, ⟶, things floating in the air move in this direction, ⟶.

Let's say a feather floating in the air goes in this direction: ⟵. Which way is the wind blowing?

The Browns Make Up a Plan

The grandmother in the Brown family gave the impression that she was very mean. She was always ordering the other Browns around. And the other Browns did a lot of yelling. But there's one thing you have to say about the Browns. They were the best hunters that ever came to Toadsville.

When fourteen Browns went running down the hill after something that looked like a great toad, it was something to see. And it was something to hear. That grandmother wasn't far away, yelling at everybody. "Come on, Billy," she'd holler.

Then she'd holler some more. "Run faster. Keep up. Don't look down, Doris. Keep your head up." When Grandmother Brown was on the east side of the lake, the people on the west side of the lake could hear everything she yelled.

After spending three days running after everything that moved, the Browns settled down. They had a plan. They didn't mention anything about what they were going to do, but everybody knew that they had a plan. People would question them. "What are you going to do?" But the Browns didn't answer these questions. The grandmother would usually say, "Stop asking questions. We've got work to do." ✦

Their plan was simple. First they stationed Browns around the places that Goad liked the most. Everybody knew where these places were. In fact, you can buy little books in the town of Toadsville that show maps of Goad's favorite spots.

The first Brown to spot Goad was Mike. When he saw Goad near the south shore of the lake, he didn't try to rush down and catch her. Instead, he motioned for the other Browns to join him. When the other Browns arrived, they put their plan into action.

They gave Goad the impression that the hills were on fire. The wind was blowing toward the lake. So six Browns lit big smoky torches. These torches made great clouds of smoke. The smoke rolled down the hills toward Goad, who was resting in the grass after eating one bee and sixteen blue flies. Goad was very smart and when she smelled the smoke, she did just what the Browns hoped she would do. She hopped toward the lake. Slowly, the fourteen Browns moved down the hill. Hop, hop. Goad moved closer to the water. As the Browns moved closer, Goad thought that the fire was coming closer. Hop, hop. Splash.

MORE NEXT TIME

E   SKILL ITEMS

Rule: **Birds have feathers.**

1.   A robin is a bird. So what does that tell you about a robin?

2.   A tiger is not a bird. So what does the rule tell you about a tiger?

3.   A jay is a bird. So what does the rule tell you about a jay?

> Use the words in the box to complete the sentences.
>
> | trouble | solid | stationed | happened | steel |
> |---|---|---|---|---|
> | propped | adults | opposite | | up |
>
> 4.   The workers ▮▮▮ ▮▮▮ the cage with ▮▮▮ bars.
> 5.   Hunters were ▮▮▮ at ▮▮▮ ends of the field.

F   REVIEW ITEMS

6.   What color are flowers that apple trees make?

7.   What grows in each place where there was a flower?

8. What do all living things need?

9. What do all living things make?

10. Do all living things grow?

11. Roots keep a tree from ▆▆▆ .

12. Roots carry ▆▆▆ to all parts of the tree.

13. When do trees begin to grow?

- in the winter
- in the spring

14. Trees begin to grow when their roots get ▆▆▆ .

15. In which seasons is the danger of forest fires greatest?

- spring and summer
- winter and spring
- summer and fall

16. The names in one box tell about time. Write the letter of that box.

17. The names in one box tell about length. Write the letter of that box.

A	month	week	year	minute	hour

B	inch	meter	mile	centimeter

END OF LESSON 21

A

1
1. twenty
2. crazy
3. fuzzy
4. exactly
5. smoky

2
1. boasting
2. roaring
3. ringing
4. screaming
5. believing
6. paddling
7. pointing

3
1. dotted
2. snapshots
3. solid
4. sticking
5. happened
6. upper

4
1. New York
2. trouble
3. impression
4. grown-ups
5. carrying
6. paddled

5
1. enough
2. engines
3. picnic
4. skip
5. unload
6. rushes

6
1. wrinkle
2. diving
3. movies
4. arrow
5. jet
6. months

B Passage 1

Names That Tell How Fast Things Move

Names that tell how fast things move have two parts. The first part of the name tells about length. The second part tells about time.

Here is a name that tells how fast things move: **centimeters per minute.** The first part of the name is **centimeters.** That part tells about length. The second part of the name is **minute.** That part tells about time.

How Air Moves an Object

In the story for today, you'll read about how air can move an object. You've seen it happen with balloons. When you fill them with air and let them go, they fly around until they run out of air.

Here's the rule about how the balloon moves: **The balloon moves the opposite direction the air moves out of the balloon.**

Touch the dotted arrow in the picture.

The dotted arrow shows the direction the air moves from the balloon.

The balloon moves the opposite direction the air moves. The solid arrow shows the direction the balloon will fly through the air.

Goad in the Water

The Browns had given Goad the impression that a fire was coming down the hill. What really came down the hill were fourteen Browns. The six grown-ups were each carrying a smoky torch. Goad went into the water, thinking that she was getting away from a fire. But she was doing just what the Browns wanted her to do. Her stubby little legs paddled her out into the lake.

When Goad was about twenty meters from the shore, the grandmother motioned to the Browns, and the Browns came roaring down the hill.

The hills were ringing with noise. Every Brown was yelling, "We've got her." But a much louder voice rang above the others. "Mark, move faster." Of course, it was Grandmother Brown, yelling orders to everybody.

It seemed that Goad would never get away from these fourteen screaming Browns. Her little legs were paddling as fast as they could, but she knew that she was in trouble. Browns were running into the water now, diving, splashing, yelling, coming at Goad like fourteen crazy people.

The next part of the story is the part that some people still have trouble believing, because there are still a lot of questions about it. Nobody has movies to show exactly what happened, but a boy from New York who was on vacation took snapshots that show what happened.

The first snapshot shows the Browns moving through the water toward Goad. In the second snapshot Goad is loading up with air. She looks like a balloon with a lot of air in it. She is almost round, with her stubby little legs sticking out to the sides. In the same picture, some of the Browns are reaching out for her.

In the third snapshot, some of the Browns are standing in the water, pointing up in the air. In the upper corner of the picture, you can see Goad, flying away from the Browns.

MORE NEXT TIME

E SKILL ITEMS

Write the word from the box that means the same thing as the underlined part of each sentence.

human	remove	horse	motion
boasting	outsmart	escape	expensive

1. That <u>person</u> can run very fast.

2. He was <u>bragging</u> about how fast he is.

3. Goad used her fourth trick to <u>get away</u> from the Browns.

4. Look at object A and object B. Write 2 ways both objects are the same.

Object A

Object B

5. Are camels used more in dry places or wet places?

6. Which animal has smooth skin, a frog or a toad?

7. Which animal can jump farther, a toad or a frog?

Some things happen as tadpoles grow.

8. Write the letter of the first change.

9. Write the letter of the last change.

  a. They grow front legs. c. They grow back legs.
  b. Their tail disappears. d. They grow a tongue.

---

10. The names in one box tell about time. Write the letter of that box.

11. The names in one box tell about length. Write the letter of that box.

  A | hour   second   year   minute   week   month

  B | inch   meter   mile   centimeter

---

12. Which has a tall straight trunk, a forest tree or an apple tree?

  • forest tree   • apple tree

13. Which has larger branches, a forest tree or an apple tree?

  • forest tree   • apple tree

14. Camel feet keep camels from sinking in sand. How are camel feet different from pig feet?
    - They are harder and longer.
    - They are sharper and smaller.
    - They are wider and flatter.

15. Where do the fleas in flea circuses usually come from?

16. What's the first thing that fleas must be taught?

END OF LESSON 22

A

1
1. moist
2. boiled
3. broiled
4. noise

2
1. <u>ba</u>ckward
2. <u>la</u>ughing
3. <u>lou</u>der
4. <u>pi</u>cnic
5. <u>lo</u>aded
6. <u>sla</u>pping

3
1. waded
2. skipped
3. soaked
4. unloaded
5. outsmarted
6. joined

4
1. gust
2. strange
3. families
4. smiled
5. crows
6. gathered
7. seeing

5
1. flight attendant
2. hamburgers
3. wrinkled
4. caught
5. completely
6. worry

6
1. greeting
2. escape
3. arrive
4. beetle
5. decide
6. beagle

Facts About Miles

The story in this lesson will tell about miles. Here are some facts about miles:

- We use miles to tell how far it is between places that are far apart.
- A mile is a little more than five thousand feet.

Look at the map. The numbers on the arrows tell how many miles it is from one place to another place.

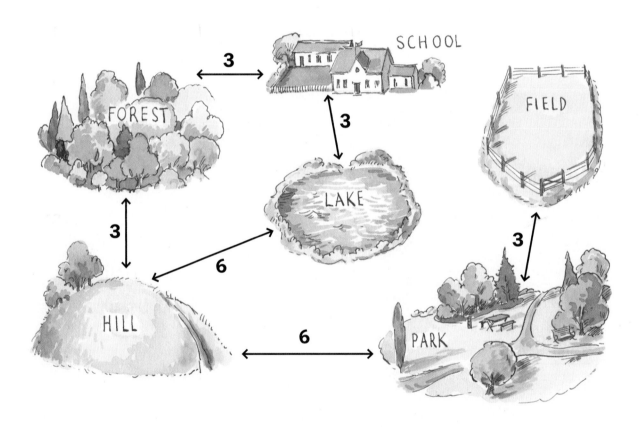

C

A Big Picnic

The three snapshots of the Browns trying to catch Goad showed Goad in the water, Goad getting bigger, and Goad flying into the air. She had loaded up with air and when the Browns were about to grab her, she unloaded.

A great gust of wind came out of her mouth, and she went flying backward. She skipped over the water two times, and then she went straight up into the air. She looked just like a great balloon when you let the air out of it. The Browns just stood there and looked.

One of the Browns said, "Oh nuts," but they seemed to know that Goad had outsmarted them. They didn't run after her. Fourteen Browns stood around in the water watching the great toad land in the weeds about a hundred meters away. Then fourteen soaked Browns waded from the water. They moved slowly.

When they joined the grandmother at the top of the hill, she did something that was very strange. She smiled. Nobody had ever seen her do that before. She had a few missing teeth, but she had a warm smile. It was the kind of old wrinkled smile that makes **you** want to smile. And that's just what happened. ✦ When she smiled, one of the little Browns smiled. Then another Brown smiled, and before you knew it, one of the soaking wet Browns began to laugh. Well, before you knew it, they were all laughing. "That's some toad," one of them yelled, and they all laughed harder.

There's something about seeing fifteen Browns laughing and slapping each other on the back. It makes you start laughing too.

A lot of people had gathered to see the Browns try to catch Goad. The first thing you know, the hills were loaded with people who were laughing. Their cheeks were moist because big tears were running down their cheeks. The sound of the laughing was very loud, but pretty soon, a much louder voice rang above the laughing. "Let's have a picnic and forget about that fat old toad."

And that's just what everybody did. All those people with binoculars and nets who had been watching. All the little kids and the families, and the old people, and dogs and cats and pet crows, and fifteen Browns. They all had a picnic. They ate boiled corn and broiled hot dogs.

They did a lot of laughing. And some people say that they could hear somebody else laughing. They say that it sounded like a laughing toad.

THE END

Number your paper from 1 through 21.

D STORY ITEMS

1. A boy from New York took three snapshots of Goad getting away from the Browns. What was Goad doing in the second snapshot?

2. What was Goad doing in the third snapshot?

3. Did the Browns catch Goad?

4. What happened right after the grandmother smiled?

   • Everybody else started yelling.

   • Three Browns started crying.

   • Some other Browns smiled.

5. Why were so many other people around the lake?

   • to see the Browns catch Goad

   • to watch the sun set

   • to see the fire

6. Write 2 things that the people ate at the picnic.

   • corn   • cake   • pie   • apples

   • chicken   • hamburgers   • hot dogs

7. Air rushes out of Goad this way ⬋ . Draw an arrow to show which way Goad will move.

8. Air rushes out of Goad this way ⬊ . Draw an arrow to show which way Goad will move.

Here's a rule: **Moles have legs like shovels.**

9. A rat is not a mole. So what does the rule tell you about a rat?

10. Joe is a mole. So what does the rule tell you about Joe?

11. Jan is not a mole. So what does the rule tell you about Jan?

12. Look at object A, object B, and object C. Write 2 ways all 3 objects are the same.

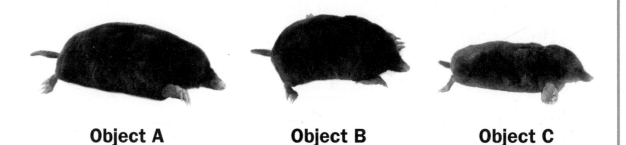

Object A   **Object B**   **Object C**

---

13. In which seasons is the danger of forest fires greatest?

   • winter and summer   • summer and fall   • fall and spring

14. Would a pig or a camel sink deeper in sand?

15. A forest fire may burn for ▨ .

   • weeks   • minutes   • hours

16. Write the letter of each statement that is make-believe.

   a. A dog can jump twenty feet high.

   b. An apple tree can talk.

   c. A forest fire can kill animals.

   d. A frog catches bugs with its tongue.

17. Which arrow shows the way the air will leave Goad's mouth?

18. Which arrow shows the way Goad will move?

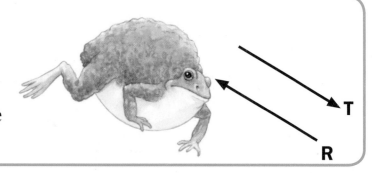

19. The names in box A tell about ▨ .

   • length   • time   • how fast things move

20. The names in box B tell about ▨ .

   • length   • time   • how fast things move

21. The names in box C tell about ▨ .

   • length   • time   • how fast things move

A
| • miles per day | • feet per minute |
| • meters per second | • meters per hour |

B | yard   inch   meter   centimeter   mile |

C | minute   year   hour   second   week   month |

END OF LESSON 23

A

1

1. mirror
2. shoe
3. Nancy
4. weigh
5. wrong
6. arrows
7. continue

2

1. completely
2. hanging
3. heavier
4. losing
5. argued
6. reached

3

1. ahead
2. apart
3. agreed
4. anyhow
5. within
6. wonder

4

1. United States
2. Lisa
3. morning
4. Saturday
5. caught
6. pulling

5

1. panting
2. worry
3. motioned
4. write
5. bridge
6. thousand
7. spoiled

6

1. mornings
2. school
3. signs
4. smiling
5. enough

More Facts About Miles

Some places are many miles apart.

- If you flew from the east side of the United States to the west side of the United States, you would go about 25 hundred miles.

- If you flew from the north side of the United States to the south side of the United States, you would go about 13 hundred miles.

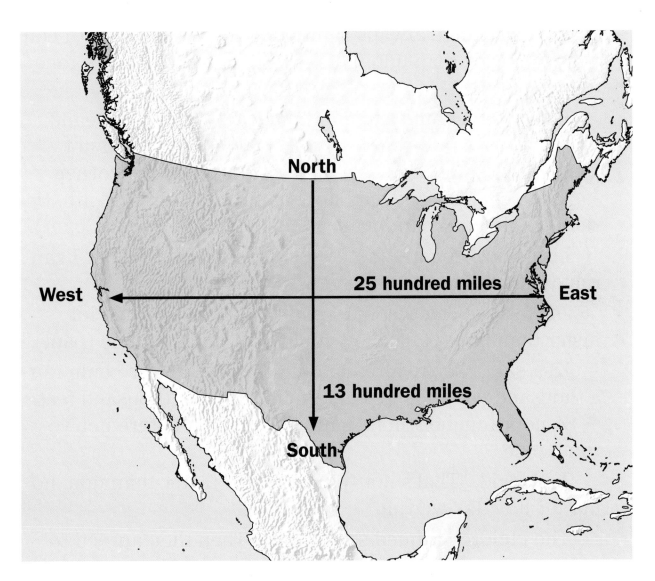

The map shows the United States.

Jack and Lisa Have a Race

Jack was two years older than his sister Lisa. Jack could do most things better than Lisa. Jack could read better and write better. Jack could lift heavier things than Lisa could lift. And Jack could run faster than Lisa.

But Lisa did something that Jack didn't do. Every morning Lisa got up and ran three miles. While Lisa was running, Jack was still sleeping.

One day Jack and Lisa were on their way to school. Jack said, "You're always running in the morning, but I can still run faster than you. I'll show you. Come on, let's race to the corner."

Before Lisa could say anything, Jack said, "Get ready. Go," and started to run. Lisa ran, too, but she could not keep up with her brother. When Lisa reached the corner, Jack was waiting and smiling, but he was out of breath. He said, "I told you (pant, pant), I could beat you (pant, pant)."

Lisa said, "You are fast in a short race, but I'll bet I can run a mile faster than you can."

Jack said, "That's a joke (pant, pant). I can run a lot faster than you (pant). So I could beat you in a mile (pant)."

Lisa said, "You're already out of breath and we only ran a thousand feet. Remember, a mile is over 5 thousand feet. ★ So your tongue will be hanging out long before you've run a mile."

Jack said, "That's not (pant) so. I'm faster than you, no matter how far we run."

The children argued some more. Then they agreed to race a mile on Saturday.

✿ On Saturday, Jack and Lisa went to a bike path near the river. They started at a place that was one mile from the big white bridge. Jack said, "By the time you get to the bridge, you'll see me there, resting in the grass."

The race started and Jack was soon far ahead of Lisa. He looked back and smiled. "Come on," he called. "Is that as fast as you can run?"

Lisa did not answer.

By the time Jack could clearly see the white bridge, he was running much slower. Lisa was now right behind him, running quite ✿ a bit faster than he was.

By the time Jack was close enough to read the large signs over the bridge, Lisa was two hundred feet ahead of him. She was pulling away, and he was panting like a sick dog.

Lisa won the race by a thousand feet. After Jack caught his breath and was able to speak without panting, he said to Lisa, "You were right. I can't run a mile as fast as you. So I'll have to start running with you in the mornings."

And that's what he did.

THE END

D SKILL ITEMS

1. Here's a rule: **The short girls run every morning.**

   Write the letters of the girls who run every morning.

   A   B   C   D   E   F

Here are titles for different stories:

   a. Liz Goes to the Zoo

   b. A Pretty New Hat

   c. The Green Dog

2. One story tells about someone who went to look at animals. Write the letter of that title.

3. One story tells about a funny-looking animal. Write the letter of that title.

4. One story tells about something you put on your head. Write the letter of that title.

5. How many centimeters long is a meter?

6. Which arrow shows the way the air will leave the jet engines?

7. Which arrow shows the way the jet will move?

8. Write the letter of every line that is one inch long.

9. Write the letter of every line that is one centimeter long.

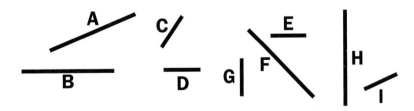

10. Write the letter of each mole.

11. Write the letter of each frog.

12. Write the letter of each toad.

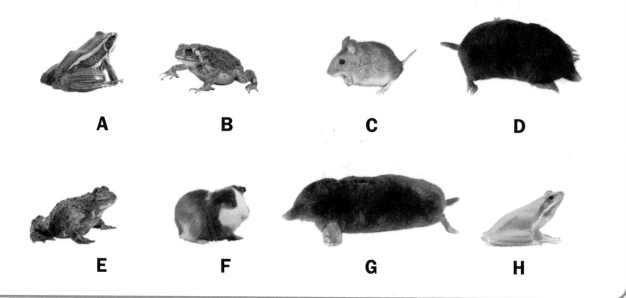

13. Name one way camel feet are different from pig feet.

14. Which letter shows where the ground gets warm first?

15. Which letter shows where the ground gets warm last?

END OF LESSON 24

A

1

1. police officer
2. horrible
3. heard
4. badge
5. edge
6. guess
7. difference

2

1. tiny
2. silly
3. thirsty
4. Nancy
5. Daddy
6. Sally

3

1. doorway
2. goodbye
3. dollhouse
4. outfit

4

1. fright
2. frighten
3. frightened
4. peanut
5. treats
6. screamed
7. shrunk

5

1. hurt
2. mirror
3. wearing
4. oil
5. kicking
6. dump
7. tight

6

1. spoiled
2. shoes
3. stamping
4. acting
5. rubbed
6. greeting
7. continued

Telling How Two Things Are Different

You're going to tell how things are different. When you tell how things are different, you must name **both** the objects you're talking about. The things in the picture are object A **and** object B. When you tell how they are different, you must name object A and object B.

Here's a sentence that does **not** tell how they are different: Object A is big. That sentence does not tell about object B.

Here's a right way of telling about that difference: Object A is big, but object B is small.

Remember, to tell one way the objects are different, you have to name **both** objects. Name another way object A and object B are different. Remember to name **both** objects.

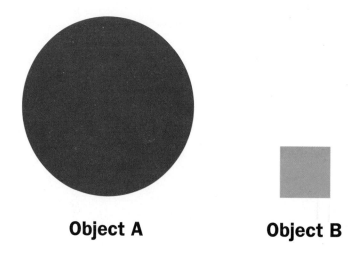

Object A   **Object B**

Nancy Wants to Stay Little

Nancy was a spoiled little girl. She liked being little because she could get her way by crying, stamping her feet, turning red in the face, and making lots of noise.

When she acted this way, her mother would say, "If you stop crying, I'll give you a treat." Nancy got lots and lots of treats by crying and acting like a little baby girl.

Then one day something happened. Nancy's dad came home from work. He picked her up and said, "How is my big girl?"

Big girl? Who wants to be a big girl? Nancy knew that if you're a big girl you can't get your way by crying and kicking and stamping and making noise.

After her dad put her down, she went to her room and looked in the mirror. She could see that what her dad said was right. She was getting bigger. The shoes she was wearing were a little tight, but when she got these shoes a few months back, they were almost too big for her. Her new striped shirt looked a little small on her.

"Oh nuts," she said in a loud voice. "I don't want to be a big girl." She kicked the mirror and hurt her foot. Then she began to cry and scream and stamp her feet and jump up and down.

That night she had a very bad dream. In her dream she was getting bigger and bigger. ✦ When she woke up the next morning she saw something on her bed. It was a note. She rubbed her eyes, picked up the note, and looked at it.

"I don't know how this note got on my bed," she said to herself. "Maybe it is something from Daddy."

Then she read the note:

> *If you hate to be tall, tall, tall,*
> *And you want to be small, small, small,*
> *Just say these words in a good loud voice:*
> *"Broil, boil, dump that oil."*

Nancy read the note two times. Then she said, "I don't know what that means."

Later that day she was playing with her friend Sally. Sally was doing tricks that Nancy couldn't do. Sally jumped rope. Then she was throwing a ball in the air and catching it.

Nancy was getting very mad because she could not do those things. At last she said, "Well, I can do something you can't do. I can make myself small by saying some words that you don't know."

"No, you can't make yourself small," Sally said.

"Yes, I can," Nancy said. "But I don't feel like doing it now."

Nancy didn't really think that she could make herself small, but she wouldn't tell that to Sally.

"You don't know any words that could make you small," Sally said.

Nancy was very mad. "Just listen to this," she said. Then she continued in a loud voice, "Broil, boil, dump that oil."

MORE NEXT TIME

D **SKILL ITEMS**

1. Which is longer, a centimeter or a meter?

2. How many centimeters long is a meter?

---

3. The names in one box tell about length. Write the letter of that box.

4. The names in one box tell about time. Write the letter of that box.

A | inch   mile   meter   centimeter |

B | month   year   hour   second   week   minute |

---

5. Which arrow shows the way the air leaves the balloon?

6. Which arrow shows the way the balloon will move?

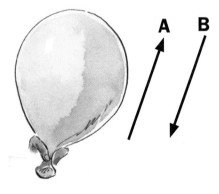

---

7. Air rushes out of Goad this way ←⎯ . Draw an arrow to show which way Goad will move.

8. What part of the world is shown on the map?

9. The map shows how far apart some places are. One line shows 13 hundred miles. The other line shows 25 hundred miles. How far is it from **R** to **T**?

10. How far is it from **M** to **K**?

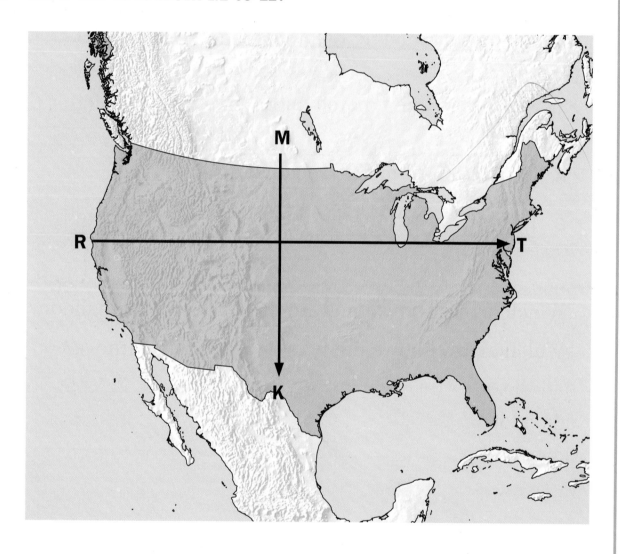

A

1
1. passenger
2. piece
3. giant
4. brought
5. cabinet
6. although
7. decide

2
1. climb
2. crumb
3. dumb
4. thumb

3
1. police officer
2. flight attendant
3. heard
4. horrible
5. badge
6. grown
7. boom

4
1. peanut
2. besides
3. sidewalk
4. bathroom
5. somehow
6. dollhouse
7. doorway

5
1. outfit
2. edge
3. shrunk
4. plastic
5. tablet
6. cookie
7. goodbye

6
1. weighed
2. holding
3. frightened
4. spinning
5. screamed
6. guessed

Facts About Ants

The story you'll read today tells about ants. Here are some facts about ants:

- Ants are insects.

  All insects have six legs.

  So ants have six legs.

- Some ants are red and some ants are black.

- Ants are very strong for their size.

Here's a rule: **An ant can carry an object that weighs ten times as much as the ant.** If an ant weighed as much as an elephant, the ant could carry ten elephants.

- Ants are very light. It would take about one hundred ants to weigh as much as a peanut.

A Green Man Visits Nancy

Nancy had just said some words that she had read on a note. All at once, the world began to spin around and around. Then Sally started to grow bigger, bigger, and bigger. Sally wasn't the only thing that began to grow. The jump rope that Sally was holding began to get larger.

Sally's voice boomed out, "Oh, what's wrong? Oh, what's wrong?" The world was still turning and spinning and things were getting larger and larger. Now Nancy was no taller than the grass next to the sidewalk.

Sally was looking down at Nancy. "Oh, Nancy, what's wrong? You're just a little tiny thing. I'll get somebody to help."

Sally dropped her jump rope and ran away. Each step that Sally took shook the ground. Nancy looked around. She was too afraid to cry. And besides, it wouldn't do any good. There was nobody around to treat her like a baby.

An ant came running along the sidewalk. When Nancy looked at the size of the ant, she knew that she had grown even smaller. To her, that ant was the size of a horse. The ant looked very mean—with its round shiny head and six legs running.

Nancy was so frightened that she screamed, but her voice did not sound like it should. Her voice had become smaller as she grew smaller. ✶ Now her voice was so small that it sounded like a little squeak. You couldn't hear her voice five meters away. "Squeak," she screamed.

At that moment, a voice behind her said, "Go away, ant."

The ant turned and ran off down the sidewalk. Nancy turned around and saw a little green man no taller than she was. "Greetings," the man said. "I am the one who left the note for you."

"Hello," Nancy said slowly. Then she said, "Why did you give me that funny note?"

The little man said, "You didn't want anybody to call you a big girl. And you got your wish. Nobody would call a tiny thing like you a big girl."

"I guess you're right," Nancy said. "But I really didn't want to be this little. I'm so little now that …"

"Now, now," the green man said. "You should be very, very happy. Even if you grow two times the size you are now, you'll be smaller than a blue fly. Even if you grow twenty times the size you are now, you'll be smaller than a mouse. So you should be very glad."

"Well, I don't …"

"I'll walk to your house with you and then I must go," the green man said. "Don't stay outside too long. There are cats and rats and loads of toads that love to eat things your size."

MORE NEXT TIME

Number your paper from 1 through 13.

D SKILL ITEMS

Here's a rule: **All the green men are small.**

1. Lee is a green man. So what does the rule tell you about Lee?

2. Jack is not a green man. So what does the rule tell you about Jack?

3. Fred is not a green man. So what does the rule tell you about Fred?

4. Write the letters of the 5 names that tell about time.

    a. meter   e. minute

    b. hour   f. week

    c. second   g. inch

    d. centimeter   h. month

5. Which animal can jump farther, a toad or a frog?

6. Which animal has smooth skin, a toad or a frog?

7. Do any frogs have teeth?

8. Write the letters of the 4 names that tell about length.

    a. week   f. minute

    b. hour   g. centimeter

    c. second   h. year

    d. mile   i. meter

    e. day   j. inch

9.   When wouldn't a fox bother a mouse?

   • during spring   • during a fire   • at night

10.   What part of the world is shown on the map?

   The map shows how far apart some places are. One line shows 13 hundred miles. The other line shows 25 hundred miles.

11.   How far is it from **A** to **B**?

12.   How far is it from **C** to **D**?

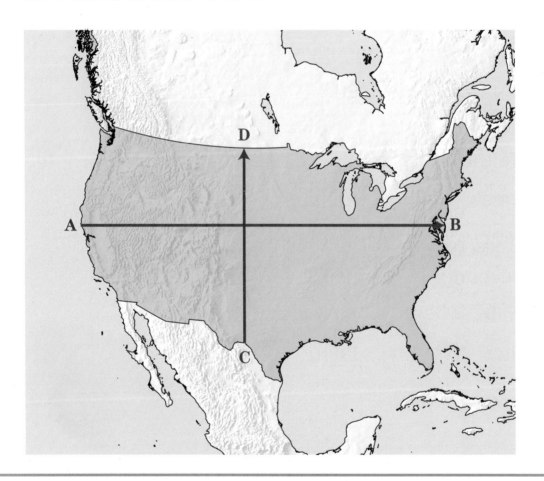

13.   A mile is a little more than ▨▨▨ feet.

   • 5 hundred   • 1 thousand   • 5 thousand

END OF LESSON 26

A

1
1. nobody
2. highest
3. napped
4. backyard
5. lowest
6. carpet
7. understand

2
1. decide
2. cabinet
3. bathroom
4. cookie
5. claim
6. nobody
7. Allen

3
1. flight attendant
2. police officer
3. plastic
4. badge
5. horrible
6. somehow
7. button

4
1. although
2. brought
3. bedroom
4. pieces
5. grain
6. tablet
7. curled

5
1. crumb
2. passengers
3. dollhouse
4. outfit
5. shrunk
6. beyond
7. lost

Nancy Is Still Tiny

The green man walked with Nancy into her house. They didn't open the door. They walked right through the crack at the bottom of the door. Then Nancy and the green man walked to Nancy's room. As soon as they were inside the room, the green man said, "Goodbye," and he left.

So there was Nancy, all alone in her room. When she had been bigger, she loved to spend time in her room. She had her dolls, her dollhouse, and her toy trains. She had a TV set, and she had a tablet. Things were not the same now that she was so small.

Nancy couldn't play with her dolls because they were at least one hundred times bigger than she was. In fact, the dollhouse was so big that Nancy almost got lost walking around inside it. She tried to turn on her TV, but she couldn't make the button move. That button was five times as big as she was.

Somehow, she made the tablet work and a great voice came from the tablet. The voice was so loud that it knocked Nancy down. "If you hate to be tall, tall, tall," the voice boomed. Nancy held her hands over her ears and tried to get away from the horrible noise. It seemed as if a long time passed before the loud voice stopped, but suddenly it was quiet in the room again.

Nancy's head hurt and she felt very tired. ★ She went back into the dollhouse and found a bed. The bed was far too big for Nancy but she curled up in a corner of the bed and took a nap.

She slept for about an hour and when she woke up, she heard voices in the room. One voice was her mother's.

The other voice belonged to a man who looked bigger than three mountains. He was dressed in a dark blue outfit, and he wore a shiny badge. Nancy's mother was crying. Nancy's mother said, "I don't know where she went. We've looked all over for her, but nobody's seen her."

The police officer said, "Now, let me make sure I understand this. The last time Nancy was seen she was playing with Sally Allen. Is that right?"

Nancy's mother said, "That's right, she was playing with Sally."

The police officer said, "And Sally Allen claims that Nancy shrunk up until she was less than one centimeter tall."

A large tear fell down and almost hit Nancy. The tear was bigger than she was. "I don't know what made Sally make up such a crazy story," Nancy's mother said. "But all I know is that my dear little Nancy is gone and I miss her. I love her very much."

"Here I am, Mom," Nancy shouted from the doorway of her dollhouse. But her voice was so small that it sounded like a tiny, tiny squeak that wasn't as loud as the sound a new shoe makes when it squeaks.

MORE NEXT TIME

Number your paper from 1 through 11.

C SKILL ITEMS

He motioned to the flight attendant ahead of him.

1. One word tells about somebody using his hands to tell a person what to do. What's that word?

2. Which two words refer to a person who takes care of passengers on a plane?

3. Which word means **in front?**

D REVIEW ITEMS

4. What do all living things need?

5. What do all living things make?

6. Do all living things grow?

7. Which arrow shows the way the air will leave the jet engines?

8. Which arrow shows the way the jet will move?

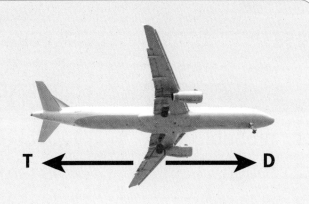

9. A mile is a little more than ▨ feet.

  • 1 thousand • 5 hundred • 5 thousand

10. If an ant weighed as much as a desk, the ant could carry an object as heavy as ▨ desks.

11. How many ants would it take to weigh as much as a peanut?

END OF LESSON 27

A

1

1. probably
2. tough
3. sweater
4. learn
5. umbrella
6. imagine
7. fist

2

1. closely
2. scary
3. easily
4. strider
5. building
6. waving
7. squeaky

3

1. wobbled
2. stretched
3. tapped
4. learned
5. decided
6. sniffed

4

1. catch your breath
2. hoist
3. crumb
4. although
5. bedroom
6. traffic
7. carpet

5

1. stale
2. cabinet
3. piece
4. grain
5. spark
6. sparkle
7. sparkled

6

1. dew
2. bathroom
3. cookie
4. beyond
5. squirrel
6. tube
7. bucket

Sugar Shines

The story you'll read today talks about how sugar shines. A grain of sugar is much smaller than an ant. It is no bigger than a grain of sand.

The picture shows what a grain of sugar would look like if it were big. The grain in the picture has corners. Each side is smooth. The sugar looks like glass. And the sugar shines like glass.

Nancy Finds Something to Eat

Nancy was shouting and waving her arms, but her mother and the police officer didn't see her as they walked from the room. Although Nancy ran as fast as her tiny legs could move, she couldn't keep up with them. By the time she reached the doorway to her bedroom, she was tired.

For her mother and the police officer, the walk to the doorway took only a few steps. But for Nancy it was a long, long run.

Nancy decided not to follow her mother beyond the bedroom door. Nancy didn't want to get lost. So she stood there trying to catch her breath.

Then she walked slowly back toward her dollhouse. On the way, she looked at all the bits and pieces of things that were stuck in the carpet. Between those giant ropes of blue and green were giant pieces of dirt and giant crumbs. One crumb was the size of a bucket next to Nancy. It was a cookie crumb. "I wonder how long it's been here," Nancy said to herself. "I wonder if it's stale." ★ She felt silly for the thought that was going through her head. She was thinking, "If that cookie crumb is any good, I'll eat the whole thing. It will be like eating the world's biggest cookie."

So she bent over and sniffed the cookie crumb. Then she tapped it with her fist. Then she broke off a little piece. That piece sparkled with shiny sugar.

Slowly, she brought the piece of cookie to her mouth and took a tiny bite from it. "Not bad," she said to herself. "Not bad at all." She took a big bite and another. With two hands she lifted up the whole crumb and began to eat it. She ate about half of it, and then she stopped. She wasn't hungry anymore.

"I need a glass of water," she said to herself. She didn't really need a glass of water. She needed much less than a drop of water. But how do you get water when you're smaller than a fly? How do you get water if you can't reach something as high as a sink? "Water," Nancy said to herself. "I must find water."

MORE NEXT TIME

Number your paper from 1 through 17.

D SKILL ITEMS

Use the words in the box to complete the sentences.

thrown	changed	stationed	motioned
opposite	wonder	flight	after	ahead

1. Hunters were ▨▨ at ▨▨ ends of the field.
2. He ▨▨ to the ▨▨ attendant ▨▨ of him.

3. In which seasons is the danger of forest fires greatest?

   - spring and summer

   - fall and winter

   - summer and fall

4. Camels can go for ▓▓▓ days without drinking water.

5. How many pounds of water can a 1 thousand-pound camel drink at one time?

6. Which is longer, one inch or one centimeter?

7. How many legs does an insect have?

8. How many legs does a flea have?

9. If a fly is an insect, what else do you know about a fly?

10. Which is longer, one centimeter or one meter?

11. How many centimeters long is a meter?

12. A toad catches flies with its ▓▓▓ .

   - tongue   - feet   - legs

13. Why do flies stick to a toad's tongue?

   - because the tongue is sticky

   - because the tongue is dirty

   - because the tongue is dry

14. If an ant weighed as much as a dog, the ant could carry an object as heavy as ▮▮▮ dogs.

15. When do trees begin to grow?

    • in the winter   • in the spring

16. Trees begin to grow when their roots get ▮▮▮ .

---

17. Camel feet keep camels from sinking in sand. How are camel feet different from pig feet?

    • They are harder and longer.

    • They are sharper and smaller.

    • They are wider and flatter.

END OF LESSON 28

A

1

1. finally
2. easily
3. closely
4. slowly
5. probably
6. early
7. badly

2

1. building
2. wobbled
3. stretched
4. thirsty
5. weighs
6. moving
7. tries

3

1. tomato
2. squirrel
3. hoist
4. tough
5. sweater
6. dew
7. scratch

4

1. forty
2. imagine
3. cover
4. discover
5. discovered
6. umbrella
7. strip

5

1. water strider
2. weren't
3. lawn
4. learn
5. tube
6. traffic
7. climbing

6

1. broken
2. hoisted
3. fallen
4. killed
5. testing
6. finished
7. windy

Passage 1

Water Has a Skin

The next story tells about the skin that water has. You can see how that skin works by filling a small tube with water. Here's a picture of what you will see.

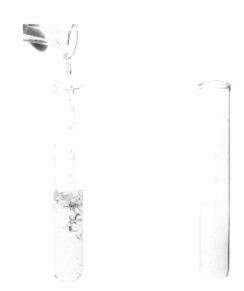

- The top of the water is not flat.
- The skin bends up in the middle.

C **Passage 2**

Facts About Dew

The story you'll read today talks about dew. The drops of water that you see on grass and cars early in the morning is called dew.

Here are some facts about dew:

- Dew forms at night.
- Dew forms when the air gets cooler.
- Dew disappears in the morning when the air warms up.

Nancy Tries to Get Some Water

✿ If Nancy knew more about very small things, she wouldn't have been so afraid of climbing to high places to find water. Here's the rule. **If tiny animals fall from high places, they don't get hurt.** If we dropped an ant from a high airplane, the ant would not be hurt at all when it landed on the ground. A mouse wouldn't be hurt either. A squirrel wouldn't be badly hurt. A dog would probably be killed. And you can imagine what would happen to an elephant.

Nancy was thirsty, so thirsty that she wanted to yell and scream and ✿ stamp her feet like a baby.

Nancy knew that it wouldn't do any good to act like a baby. So she made up her mind to start thinking. She was pretty smart. She said to herself, "If it were early morning, I could go out and drink dew from the lawn." But the grass was not moist with dew, and Nancy couldn't wait until morning.

So she went to the bathroom, looking for water.

She had walked from her bedroom to the bathroom hundreds of times before, but this time it wasn't a walk. It was a long, long trip. She finally arrived in the bathroom. She walked around as she made up a plan for getting water. ✦ Here's the plan: She would climb up the corner strip of the cabinet. That strip was made of rough wood and it was easy to grip. It went straight to the top of the cabinet.

Nancy didn't know what kind of problem would meet her at the top of the cabinet. But first she had to get to the top. So up she went. She hoisted herself up one centimeter, two centimeters. Slowly, up. Then she began moving faster and faster. "This isn't too hard," she said to herself. When she was almost at the top, she reached a spot where the strip was moist with oil. And she slipped. She fell all the way to the floor.

The fall scared her. She landed on her back. For a moment she didn't move. Then she got up slowly, testing her arms and legs to make sure that they weren't hurt. She had fallen from something that was a hundred times taller than she was, but she wasn't hurt. She wasn't hurt at all, not one broken bone. Not one scratch. Not even an ouch.

"I don't know what's happening," Nancy said to herself. "But I'm not afraid to try climbing that cabinet again."

This time she got to the top.

MORE NEXT TIME

Number your paper from 1 through 13.

E SKILL ITEMS

Here's a rule: **Horses eat grass.**

1. A cow is not a horse. So what does the rule tell you about a cow?

2. Jake is not a horse. So what does the rule tell you about Jake?

3. Meg is a horse. So what does the rule tell you about Meg?

F REVIEW ITEMS

4. Roots keep a tree from ▮▮ .

5. Roots carry ▮▮ to all parts of the tree.

6. Camels can go for ▮▮ days without drinking water.

7. How many pounds of water can a 1 thousand-pound camel drink at one time?

8. What part of the world is shown on the map?

The map shows how far apart some places are. One line shows 13 hundred miles. The other line shows 25 hundred miles.

9. How far is it from **F** to **G**?

10. How far is it from **H** to **K**?

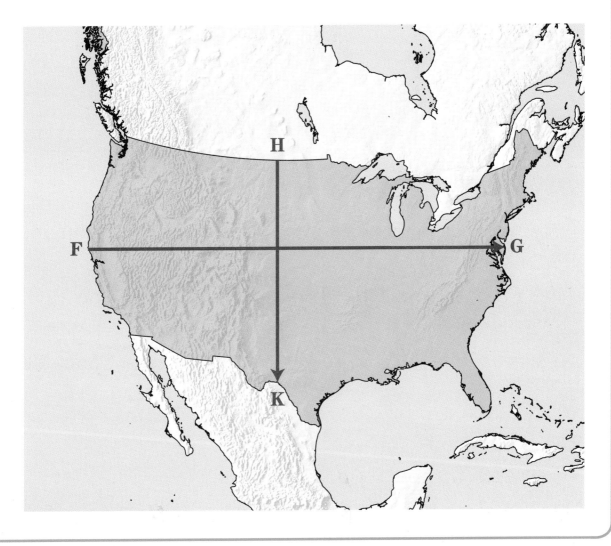

11. If a grain of sugar were very big, it would look like a box made of ▨ .

Some of the lines in the box are one inch long and some are one centimeter long.

12. Write the letter of every line that is one centimeter long.

13. Write the letter of every line that is one inch long.

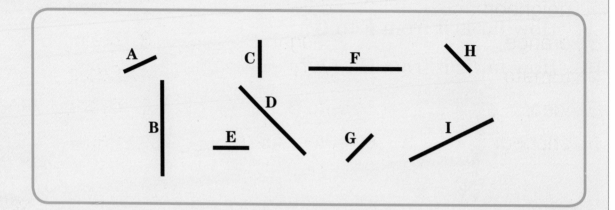

A

1
1. supposed to be
2. neighborhood
3. orange
4. tomato
5. idea
6. shaped

2
1. rocking chair
2. riddle
3. thought
4. worm
5. retold
6. remembered

3
1. ago
2. bored
3. boring
4. Eddie
5. Granny
6. Papa

4
1. questions
2. answers
3. square
4. squeaky
5. leftover
6. finding

5
1. make sense
2. puzzle
3. solve
4. solved
5. walnut
6. porch

6
1. chimney
2. center
3. cone
4. carrot
5. celery
6. coconut

The Little Red House

A story retold by Wolfgang Engelmann
Illustrated by Loyal de Neuville

A long time ago, there was a seven-year-old boy named Eddie. He was bored one day, and told his mother, "I'm bored. What can I do that is not boring?"

His mother said, "You can do something for me."

Eddie said, "What is that?"

She smiled and said, "You can bring me a little red, round house with no windows, no doors, a chimney on top, and a star inside."

The boy thought about that, but it didn't make any sense. He said, "Houses aren't round. And how could you get in or out of the house if it didn't have windows or doors? And how could a star get inside the house?"

With a smile she said, "Well, you'll have to find that out. I'll be waiting for you to bring a little red house to me."

Eddie went outside and was looking around his neighborhood, trying to find a little round, red house when he met a girl. He asked her if she knew where he could find "A little red, round house with no windows, no doors, a chimney on top, and a star inside."

She said, "I've seen houses that are little and houses that are square, but I've never seen a little house that is round. Maybe my papa knows. He's a very smart farmer."

So Eddie and the girl walked to the farm, and walked up to the farmer. The little girl said, "Papa, this little boy needs help finding something."

The farmer asked, "What's that?"

Eddie said, "Have you ever seen a little red, round house with no windows, no doors, a chimney on top, and a star inside?"

The farmer thought and shook his head. He said, "I've seen red barns, and maybe a red house or two, but I've never seen a round house with no doors or windows."

Eddie was ready to go back home when the farmer said, "But here's an idea. Go down the road to the next house. Granny lives there. She's very old and she's seen just about everything there is to see. Maybe she knows the answer."

Eddie thanked the farmer and the girl. Then he ran down the road to the next house. Granny was on the porch rocking in a rocking chair. Eddie ran up to her and asked, "Granny, do you know how I could find a little red, round house with no windows, no doors, a chimney on top, and a star inside?"

She rocked and rocked for a while, not saying anything, just thinking. Then she said, "I've never seen anything like that, but I'd sure like to be inside a house with a star after the sun goes down." Granny rocked some more, then she stopped again and said, "You go back to the road and ask the wind if it knows where to find that house."

"The wind?" Eddie asked. "I've never talked to the wind."

Granny said, "Well, then it's time you did. Go back to the road and tell the wind about the little red house."

Eddie ran to the road, held his arms out and shouted, "Wind! Wind! Have you seen a little red, round house with no windows, no doors, a chimney on top, and a star inside?"

Nothing happened for a while. Then Eddie felt the wind on his back, pushing him to show where he should go. He walked forward, and the wind continued to push. When he was pretty far from Granny's house, the wind stopped and Eddie stopped. He shouted, "Wind! I don't see the little red house."

The wind blew against his side, showing him which way to go. He went a few steps, but then he had to stop because a big apple tree was in his way. When he looked at the tree, the wind stopped.

Eddie thought, "Maybe the wind is telling me this is where I should be."

Suddenly a sharp wind blew in Eddie's face. It blew a red apple from the tree. The apple rolled up to his shoe and stopped.

He slowly picked it up and said, "It's little. It's red. And it's round."

He still had some questions, but he said, "This may be what I'm looking for." He ran all the way back home with the apple. He remembered to thank Granny as he ran past her house.

When he got home, he showed the apple to his mother and said, "Is this the little house?"

She laughed and said, "Yes, it is."

He asked, "But Mom, where is the star inside?"

She went into the kitchen, put the apple on its side and cut it in half. In the middle of each half was a star.

"Wow," Eddie said, "It's little, it's red, it's round, it's even got a chimney, and a star inside, but it's supposed to be a house. Who would want to live inside an apple?"

Just then two tiny green worms stuck their heads out of the chimney of the apple and said something in squeaky little voices. Eddie thought he heard them say, "We love our house."

Number your paper from 1 through 11.

C STORY ITEMS

1. Why did Eddie's mother give him a riddle to solve?

2. What was the riddle?

3. Eddie asked a lot of people about the puzzle. Name 3 of those people.

4. Who did Granny tell him to ask?

5. How did the wind lead him to the place where he would find the answer to the riddle?

6. What was the answer to the riddle?

D SKILL ITEMS

Write the correct word or letter to complete each sentence.

star	C	cone	X	sun	S	lake

7. An **egg** is a house with a part that is something like the ▨ .

8. A **coconut** is a house with a ▨ in the center.

9. An **apple** is a house with a ▨ inside.

10. A **carrot** is shaped like a plate if you look at it one way. It's shaped like a ▨ if you look at it another way.

11. A **celery** stick is shaped like an **I** if you look at it one way. It's shaped like the letter ▨ if you look at it another way.

Pick two of the pictures with your partner. Write a riddle for each of those pictures on a new piece of paper.

Walnut

Orange

Tomato

Peach

Sun

END OF LESSON 30

A

1

1. unit
2. search
3. complain
4. refrigerator
5. supposed
6. decision
7. couple

2

1. stretched
2. discovered
3. weighed
4. finished
5. learned

3

1. housefly
2. beetles
3. darkness
4. umbrella
5. frightened
6. wondering

4

1. easily
2. strider
3. scary
4. blank
5. sweater
6. dents

5

1. wrist
2. hunger
3. gram
4. tough
5. scale
6. neck

6

1. tugged
2. backed
3. climbed
4. touched
5. charged

More About the Skin That Water Has

When we fill a tube with water, you can see that the water has a skin. You can use a dish of water and a hair to show that water has a skin.

First you can float a hair on water. If you're careful, the hair won't even get wet. It will just rest on the skin of the water.

Hair A in the picture is resting on the water.

Look at hair B. The end of that hair is pushed down through the skin of the water. As the hair goes down, the skin of the water bends down around the hair. Look at the skin around hair B.

The end of hair C is under the water. But hair C is moving up. When the hair moves up slowly, the skin hangs on to the hair and bends up. Remember, when the hair goes up, the skin bends up. When the hair goes down, the skin bends down.

Nancy Gets Some Water

Nancy had climbed to the top of the cabinet. She was ready to have a nice drink of water. Next to the sink there were lots of drops of water. Some drops were bigger than she was. Some drops were about the size of an open umbrella top. She rushed over to them.

Nancy didn't know much about water drops. Here's the rule: **Water drops have a skin that goes all the way around them.** That skin is tough. If you are at a pond, you may see little insects called water striders that walk right on top of the water. They are walking on the skin of the water.

If you look closely, you can see that the legs of water striders make little dents in the water but their legs do not go into the water. The legs just bend the skin of the water down without going through the skin.

Nancy had seen water striders, but she didn't think about how tough the skin of water must be if you are very small. She ran over to one drop of water. The drop of water came up to her knees. Then she bent over and touched the water drop with her hands. It felt like a water balloon.

When she pushed, the skin moved in. But her hands didn't go through the skin. ✦ "How do insects drink water?" she thought to herself. Then she got back to her problem. "How am I going to drink?"

"I'll just hit it harder," she thought. She made a fist and hit the drop as hard as she could. Her fist went right through the skin of the drop. Her hand was wet and her arm was wet. She pulled her hand back, but it didn't come out easily. It stuck at the wrist.

She pulled and tugged, and the skin of the water stretched out. Finally, **pop.** Her hand came out, and the skin of the drop wobbled back into its round shape.

Nancy thought about the best way of getting water from the drop. At last, she backed up a few steps, put her head down, and charged the drop of water. Her head hit the water drop and **pop.** Her head went through the skin.

She drank quickly, trying not to get water in her nose. Then she pulled her head back. The skin of the water tugged at her neck. The water pulled at her neck the way a tight sweater pulls on your neck when you try to take it off. Nancy pulled hard, and **pop.** Her head came out of the drop.

"That was scary," she said out loud.

MORE NEXT TIME

Number your paper from 1 through 23.

STORY ITEMS

1. Some drops of water were ▨▨▨ than Nancy.

   • bigger   • older   • hotter

2. When Nancy first touched the water drop, did her hand get wet?

3. What did Nancy have to do to get her hand inside the water drop?

   - look at the drop
   - hit the drop
   - touch the drop

4. Did Nancy get her head inside the water drop?

5. What happened when Nancy tried to pull her head back out of the water drop?

   - It got smaller.
   - It got stuck.
   - It got wet.

6. Write the letters of the water striders.

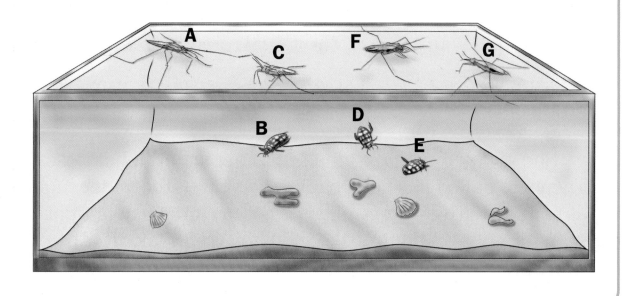

List the 4 things that Nancy has learned about being very small.

7. Small animals have a voice that is ▩ .

8. Small animals don't get hurt when they ▩ .

9. Water has a ▩ .

10. A loud sound can ▩ a small animal.

11. Is a water strider an insect?

12. How many legs does a water strider have?

13. How many legs does an ant have?

14. How many legs does a spider have?

15. How many legs does a flea have?

16. How many legs does a cat have?

E SKILL ITEMS

17. Write one way that tells how both objects are the same.

18. Write 2 ways that tell how object A is different from object B.

Object A

Object B

Write the word from the box that means the same thing as the underlined part of each sentence.

heard	hoisted	long	sale
lawn	silly	boomed	stale

19. The cake was <u>old and not very good to eat</u>.

20. The <u>grass</u> was wet after the rain.

21. They <u>lifted</u> the TV onto the truck.

F REVIEW ITEMS

22. The names in one box tell about time. Write the letter of that box.

23. The names in one box tell about length. Write the letter of that box.

A | centimeter   inch   meter   mile

B | week   year   second   month   minute   hour

END OF LESSON 31

A

1
1. discovered
2. wondered
3. finished
4. complained
5. learned
6. supposed

2
1. <u>house</u>flies
2. <u>fo</u>rever
3. <u>base</u>ball
4. <u>foot</u>ball

3
1. stale
2. grams
3. search
4. moving
5. traffic

4
1. decision
2. refrigerator
3. weighs
4. dining
5. chunk
6. blanks

5
1. lawn
2. hoist
3. reply
4. replied
5. thirty

6
1. scrap
2. couple
3. hunger
4. toast
5. unit
6. forty

B

Grams

In some stories, you've read about things that do not weigh very much. When we weigh very small things, the unit we use is grams.

Here's a rule about grams: **All grams are the same weight.**

If you had a block of water that was one centimeter on all sides, that block would weigh one gram.

A pencil weighs more than a gram. A long pencil weighs about five grams. A short pencil weighs about two grams.

C

Nancy Is Hungry Again

Nancy found out four things about being very small. She found out that small things have very high voices. She also learned that if you are very small, a loud sound can knock you down. She also discovered that very small things do not hurt themselves when they fall from high places. The fourth thing she discovered was that a drop of water is very different to someone who is quite small.

During her first night of being small, Nancy found out a fifth fact about being small. Here's the rule: **The food that a very small animal eats each day weighs more than the animal.**

Let's say a small animal weighs one gram. The food that the animal eats each day weighs more than one gram. The food that bigger animals eat each day does not weigh as much as the animals. An elephant may eat two hundred pounds of food each day, but the elephant may weigh more than a thousand pounds. An adult human may eat five pounds of food each day, but the adult weighs much more than five pounds. A large dog may eat three pounds of food every day but the dog may weigh more than 80 pounds. ★

Nancy learned this rule during the first night that she was very small. She woke up in the middle of the night. She was very hungry. So she got up from her dollhouse bed and went looking for another chunk of cookie that was on her rug. She found one and ate it. Then she felt thirsty, so she went back to the bathroom, climbed to the top of the cabinet, and drank from a drop of water.

"That's scary," she said when she finished.

She went back to bed in her dollhouse, but before the sun came up, she woke up again. She was hungry. The cookie crumbs were gone so she couldn't eat cookie crumbs. She tried to forget about how hungry she was. She knew that she had already eaten a chunk of cookie that weighed almost as much as she did. She wondered, "How can I still be hungry?"

The feeling of hunger did not go away. After a few minutes, she got out of bed. "Oh nuts," she said. "I'm going to have to go hunting for food."

MORE NEXT TIME

Number your paper from 1 through 14.

D SKILL ITEMS

1. Write one way that tells how both objects are the same.

2. Write 2 ways that tell how object A is different from object B.

Object A   **Object B**

The traffic was moving 27 miles per hour.

3. How fast was the traffic moving?

4. If the traffic was moving 27 miles per hour, how far would a car go in one hour?

5. What word in the sentence refers to all the cars and trucks that were moving on the street?

6. What word means **each?**

7. Which arrow shows the way the air leaves the balloon?

8. Which arrow shows the way the balloon will move?

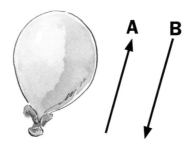

9. Write the letters of the 4 names that tell about length.

a. minute	d. centimeter	g. mile	j. inch
b. hour	e. second	h. meter	k. month
c. day	f. week	i. year	

Look at the skin around each hair.

- Make an arrow like this ↑ if the hair is moving up.
- Make an arrow like this ↓ if the hair is moving down.

10.   11.   12.   13.   14.

END OF LESSON 32

A

1
1. instead
2. couple
3. expression
4. important

2
1. soundly
2. moments
3. wondering
4. frightened
5. baseballs
6. counter

3
1. full-sized
2. forever
3. refrigerator
4. footballs
5. decision
6. answered

4
1. chunk
2. search
3. scale
4. cherry
5. toast
6. scraps

5
1. yourself
2. whirl
3. swirl
4. learned
5. dining
6. stuff
7. thick

More About Grams

You learned about grams. You know that grams are used to weigh some kinds of things. You know how much water it takes to weigh one gram. You know how much a long pencil weighs. You know how much a short pencil weighs. Here are some facts about how much other things weigh. A big cherry weighs about ten grams. An apple weighs about two hundred grams.

Most insects weigh much less than a gram. Even a very big spider like the spider in the picture weighs less than a gram.

It would take about one hundred ants to weigh one gram.

It would take about thirty houseflies to weigh one gram.

It would take about two hundred fleas from Russia to weigh one gram.

The picture below shows how much a big beetle weighs. How many grams of water are on the scale?

So how much weight is on the side of the scale with the beetle?

Nancy Finds Some More Food

Nancy went toward the kitchen. The walk seemed to take forever. The house was dark and Nancy couldn't see well, so she felt the walls and walked slowly toward the kitchen. When she was in the dining room, she could hear the sound of the refrigerator. In fact, she could feel the refrigerator. It shook the floor.

Finally, Nancy reached the kitchen. By now, she was so hungry that she wanted to scream and cry and kick and roll around on the floor like a baby. But she didn't do any of those things because she knew that acting like a baby wouldn't do any good. So she opened her eyes wide and tried to look for scraps of food.

Near the refrigerator, she found something. She bent over and sniffed it. She wasn't sure what it was, but it smelled bad. "I'm not that hungry," she said. "I'll bet that chunk of food has been on the floor for a week."

Nancy walked nearly all the way around the kitchen, but she couldn't find any other food. "I'll bet there's food on the counter," she said to herself.

Up she went, without feeling frightened. She reached the top and began to search the counter. ✦

She smelled it before she saw it—toast. She followed her nose. In the darkness, she could just see the toast. Four pieces of toast were piled on a plate. To Nancy, the pile of toast looked like a giant ten-story building.

Nancy was wondering how to climb onto the plate so that she could reach the toast. But when she started to walk around the plate, she found crumbs all over the counter. There were crumbs that seemed as big as baseballs and crumbs as big as footballs. There was even one crumb that was the size of a chair.

Nancy picked up a crumb that was the size of a football. She ate it with a loud, "Chomp, chomp, chomp."

When Nancy had been full-sized, she hated toast. She complained when her mother served it. "Oh, not that stuff," she used to say. "I hate toast."

Now that she was small and hungry all the time, she didn't hate toast. In fact, that crumb of toast tasted so good that she ate another piece the size of a football.

Nancy weighed much less than a gram. In one day, she had eaten food that weighed a gram.

MORE NEXT TIME

D INFORMATION ITEMS

1. Does a housefly weigh more than a gram or less than a gram?

2. Does a glass of water weigh more than a gram or less than a gram?

3. How many ants would it take to weigh one gram?

4. There is one gram on the left side of the scale. So how much weight is on the side of the scale with the water striders?

5. Which weighs more, one gram or one water strider?

E REVIEW ITEMS

6. Write the letters of the 4 names that tell about time.

    a. week   b. inch   c. centimeter   d. second

    e. minute   f. meter   g. hour

7. If a grain of sugar were very big, it would look like a box made of ▩ .

8. When we weigh very small things, the unit we use is ▩ .

9. The food that 3 of the animals eat each day weighs as much as those animals. Write the letters of those animals.

10. The food that 4 of the animals eat each day does not weigh as much as those animals. Write the letters of those animals.

A

1
1. neither
2. remind
3. manage
4. prove

2
1. answered
2. learned
3. worried
4. managed

3
1. become
2. yourself
3. soundly
4. darling
5. instead

4
1. whirl
2. couple
3. moments
4. important
5. expression

5
1. tight
2. tightly
3. thick
4. sobbing
5. swirl

The Green Man Visits Nancy Again

Nancy was full. She didn't feel like climbing down from the counter top, so she just jumped. For Nancy, it was like jumping from the top of a building that is more than one hundred stories tall. But she landed on her feet as easily as you would if you jumped from a chair to the floor. She walked back to her dollhouse. By the time she got back in bed, it was almost time for the sun to come up. She wasn't very tired, but she made a decision to sleep. She closed her eyes, and in a few moments, she was sleeping soundly.

"Wake up, wake up," a loud voice said. Nancy opened her eyes. For a moment she didn't know where she was or what was standing in front of her. It was green and it was speaking in a loud voice, "Come on and wake up. Wake up."

"I'm awake," Nancy said. Her voice sounded thick and sleepy. The room was light. In fact, things looked so bright that Nancy had to cover her eyes. "Is that you?" she asked.

✿ The little green man answered, "Of course it's me. I've come to see if you're happy."

"No, I'm not happy," Nancy said.

"And why not?" the green man asked. ✦

"Because I don't like being so little."

"Oh," the green man said and sat down. "I thought you never wanted to get big."

"I was wrong," Nancy replied. "I want to get big. I want to grow up. I want to be back with my parents and my friends."

The little green man said, "I can change you back to your regular size if I want to. But I'm not going ✿ to change you unless you tell me some things that you learned." The green man stood up and stared at Nancy. "What have you learned about kicking and screaming and acting like a baby?"

Nancy smiled. "I don't have to act like a baby because I can take care of myself."

The man said, "And when nobody is around, what do you do instead of kicking and crying?"

Nancy said, "You have to take care of yourself."

"Good," the green man said. "I'm glad that you learned things about yourself. But have you learned things about the world you live in?"

"Lots of things," Nancy said, and she began to list them. "I've learned that little things don't hurt themselves when they fall from high places. I've learned that…" Suddenly everything seemed to whirl and swirl around. Nancy tried to keep talking. "I've learned …" She felt very dizzy.

MORE NEXT TIME

Number your paper from 1 through 20.

Write the word from the box that means the same thing as the underlined part of each sentence.

hoist	fish	tadpoles	squeak
remove	climb	moist	wrong

1. The pond is full of <u>baby frogs</u>.

2. The grass is <u>a little wet</u> today.

3. She will <u>take</u> the books from the desk.

Some things happen as tadpoles grow.

4. Write the letter of what happens first.

5. Write the letter of what happens last.

    a. They grow front legs.   c. They turn blue.

    b. Their tail disappears.   d. They grow back legs.

6. The picture shows Goad filled up with air. Arrow A shows air leaving Goad this way ⟶.

Write the letter of the arrow that shows the way Goad will move.

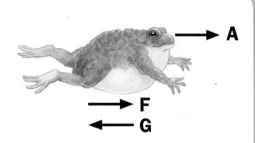

7. A mile is a little more than ▮▮ feet.

   • 2 thousand   • 5 thousand   • 1 thousand

8. If an ant weighed as much as a cat, the ant could carry an object as heavy as ▮▮ .

These animals fell from a high place. Write the words that tell what happened to each animal.

| not hurt | hurt | killed |

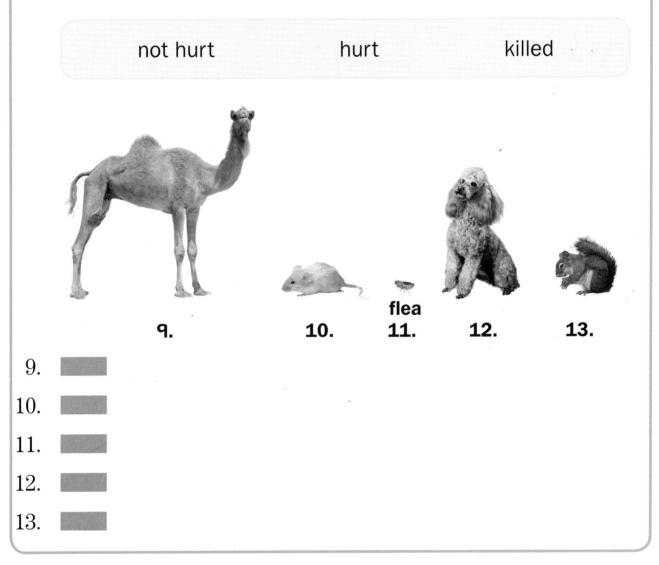

9.   10.   flea 11.   12.   13.

9. ▮▮
10. ▮▮
11. ▮▮
12. ▮▮
13. ▮▮

14. Does a housefly weigh more than a gram or less than a gram?

15. Does a dog weigh more than a gram or less than a gram?

16. How many grams are on the left side of the scale?

17. So how much weight is on the side of the scale with the houseflies?

1 gram

18. An arrow goes from the **F.** Which direction is that arrow going?

19. An arrow goes from the **G.** Which direction is that arrow going?

20. An arrow goes from the **J.** Which direction is that arrow going?

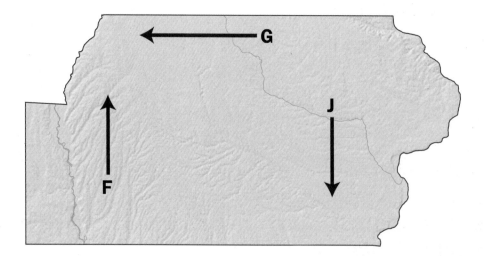

END OF LESSON 34

A

1
1. several
2. continue
3. distance
4. sobbing
5. worried
6. couple

2
1. desk
2. prove
3. instead
4. managed
5. reminds

3
1. canoe
2. expression
3. darling
4. neither
5. becoming
6. important

4
1. threw
2. tightly
3. nor
4. swirling
5. snaps

B

Sounds That Objects Make

In lesson 26 you read about Nancy's voice and what happened to it when she became smaller and smaller. Here's the rule about your voice: **If you get smaller, your voice gets higher.**

Follow these instructions and you will see how sounds get higher when things get smaller.

1. Place a plastic ruler so that one end of it is on your desk and the other end hangs over the edge of the desk. Make sure that most of the ruler hangs over the desk. The picture shows how to place the ruler on your desk.

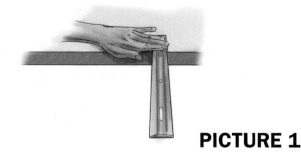

PICTURE 1

2. Hold down the end of the ruler that is on the desk.
3. Bend the other end of the ruler down. Then let it go so it snaps back. The ruler will make a sound.

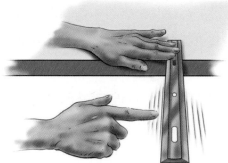

PICTURE 2

4. Now move the ruler so a smaller part of the ruler hangs over the edge of the desk. The ruler will make a sound that is higher.
5. Now move the ruler so that even less of the ruler hangs over the edge of the desk. The ruler will make a sound that is even higher.

The ruler works just like your voice. When your body gets smaller, the sound of your voice gets higher.

Nancy Becomes Regular Size

The whole room seemed to be turning and swirling. Nancy felt so dizzy that she was afraid she would fall over. She kept trying to tell the little green man about the things she had learned. Finally, she managed to say, "I learned that water has a skin."

Nancy closed her eyes and talked very loudly. She hoped that she could stop the dizzy feeling by talking loudly.

Suddenly, Nancy opened her eyes. But she didn't see the little green man. She saw the face of a woman.

The expression on that woman's face was one of shock. Her eyes were wide open and so was her mouth. "Where …," the woman said, "where have you been?"

The expression changed. Tears began to form in the woman's eyes. Then Nancy's mother threw her arms around Nancy and picked her up. "Oh, Nancy," she said. Her voice was sobbing, and she was holding Nancy very tightly. "Oh, darling," she said. "We've been so worried …"

Nancy started to cry. She didn't want to cry, but she was so glad to see her mother, and it felt so good to have her mother hold her. She couldn't hold back the tears. "Oh, Mother," she said.

Nancy's mother held her for a long time. ✦ For a few minutes, after her mother set her down, neither Nancy nor her mother said anything. Then, her mother grabbed Nancy's hands and held them tightly as she said, "Nancy, where have you been? The police have been looking for you and … And Sally told a crazy story about you becoming very small."

"It's true," Nancy said. "I know it sounds crazy, but I can prove to you that it really happened. I can tell you where the crumbs of toast are on the counter. I can tell you about the drops of water in the bathroom." Nancy said. "And I can tell you other things."

Nancy's mother was smiling and crying and laughing at the same time. "Oh, Nancy, I don't know what to believe, but I'm very glad to have my darling little baby back."

Nancy said, "I'm not a baby. That's the most important thing I learned when I was less than one centimeter tall. I can take care of myself. And I don't mind growing up at all."

That story took place a couple of years ago. Nancy is still growing up. And she's doing a fine job. She doesn't act like a baby—not even when things go wrong. Instead, she reminds herself, "I can take care of myself." And that's just what she does.

THE END

Number your paper from 1 through 24.

D SKILL ITEMS

He is supposed to make a decision in a couple of days.

1. What part means **should?**

2. What word means **two?**

3. What part means **make up his mind?**

4. Write one way that tells how both objects are the same.

5. Write 2 ways that tell how object A is different from object B.

Object A   **Object B**

Some of the lines in the box are one inch long and some are one centimeter long.

6. Write the letter of every line that is one inch long.

7. Write the letter of every line that is one centimeter long.

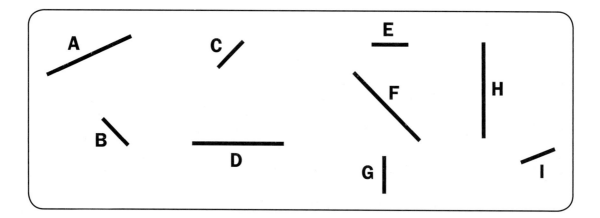

8. Which arrow shows the way the air will leave the jet engines?

9. Which arrow shows the way the jet will move?

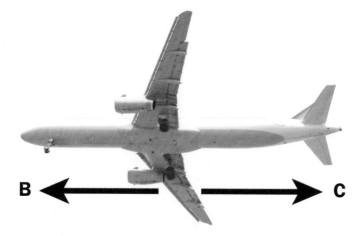

10. Write the letter of each water strider.

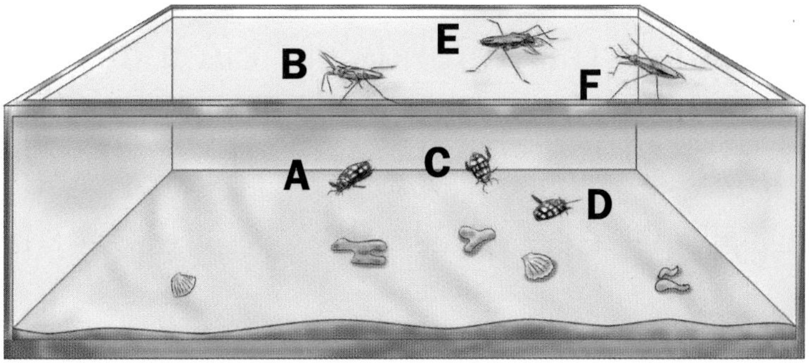

11. Is a water strider an insect?
12. How many legs does a water strider have?
13. How many legs does a fly have?
14. How many legs does a dog have?
15. How many legs does a spider have?
16. How many legs does an ant have?
17. When we weigh very small things, the unit we use is ______ .

Some things in the picture weigh **1 gram.** Some weigh **2 grams.** Some weigh **5 grams.** Write how much each object weighs.

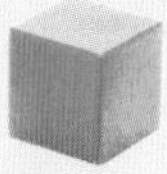

18.

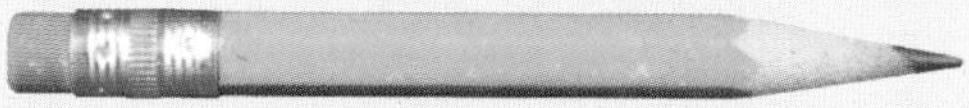

19.

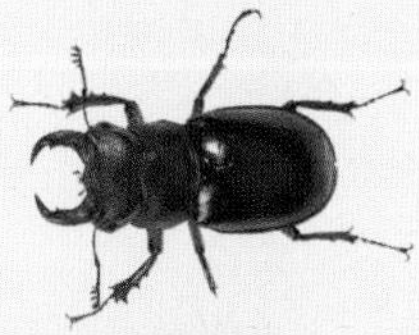

20.

21.

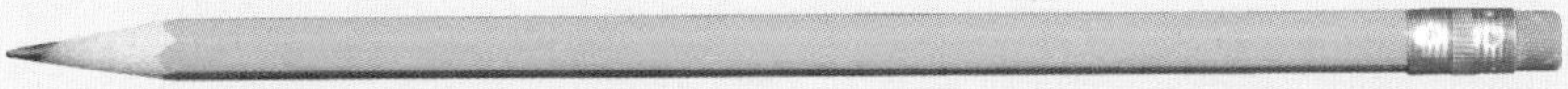

22.

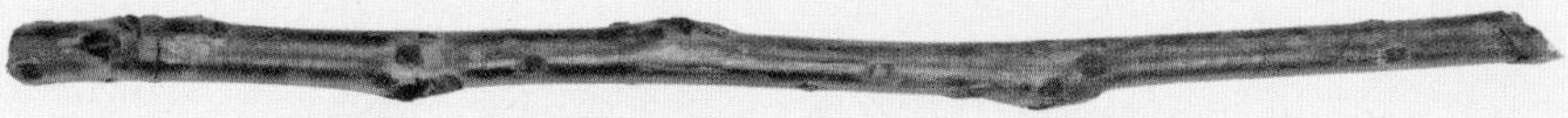

23. The food that 3 of the animals eat each day weighs more than those animals. Write the letters of those animals.

24. The food that 4 of the animals eat each day does not weigh as much as those animals. Write the letters of those animals.

Vocabulary Sentences

Lessons 1–35

1. You measure your weight in pounds.

2. They waded into the stream to remove tadpoles.

3. The fly boasted about escaping from the spider.

4. The workers propped up the cage with steel bars.

5. Hunters were stationed at opposite ends of the field.

6. He motioned to the flight attendant ahead of him.

7. The traffic was moving forty miles per hour.

8. He is supposed to make a decision in a couple of days.